REDISCOVERING PRAYER

REDISCOVERING PRAYER

John R. Yungblut

Rockport, Massachusetts • Shaftesbury, Dorset

Published in the U.S.A. in 1991 by
Element, Inc.
42 Broadway, Rockport, MA 01966

Published in Great Britain in 1991 by
Element Books Limited
Longmead, Shaftesbury, Dorset

Cover design by Max Fairbrother

Cover illustration by Giotto, courtesy of SCALA

Printed and bound in the U.S.A. by
Edwards Brothers, Inc.

Library of Congress Catalog Card Number available
ISBN 1–85230–265–8

ACKNOWLEDGMENTS

Grateful acknowledgment is made to the following publishers for permission to use copyrighted material from the authors and titles listed:

Harcourt, Brace, Jovanovich, Inc.,—T. S. Eliot, *The Waste Land and Other Poems.*

Harper & Row, Inc.—Pierre Teilhard de Chardin, *The Divine Milieu* and *The Phenomenon of Man.*

Little, Brown and Company—C. G. Jung, *The Undiscovered Self.*

PREFACE

THERE ARE THOUSANDS, perhaps millions, of men and women who still pray, much as church members have prayed for a millennium. The charisma of the institution still holds them in thrall. Without hesitation they embrace the doctrines of the Church; the Christ myth seizes them and shapes the pattern of their thought. It is enough that the historic Jesus commanded them to pray. Not to respond in obedience would be to stand under judgment. I respect them.

I have sometimes wished it were possible for me also to accept the doctrines of the Church in a literal sense and to build a bastion in the mind against doubt and eternal questioning, search and research. But that way has been closed to me and, I suspect, closed for an ever-increasing number of my fellows. For us, doctrines of the Church need constantly to be re-examined, as the metaphors they are, for a reality which, like God himself, resists all forms of idolatry, even including uncritical profession of literal belief. All the great metaphors of the faith must be tried in the crucible of present experience and reflection to determine in what sense they are still viable as metaphors and in what sense they need to be submitted to continued revision, restatement, or replacement.

There are two new perspectives to which modern man is heir: the evolutionary and the depth-psychological. It is my conviction that no man whose thinking is not yet radically affected by these can be said to be fully modern. These perspectives are, of course, interrelated. The evolutionary is the inclusive one. The depth-psychological may be thought of as one of its corollaries as applied to the human psyche. Modern man is at once both post-Darwinian and post-Freudian, and in some profound sense this fact can be said to make all the difference. Therefore, what I shall say in the chapters that follow is addressed primarily to those men and women who recognize that their thinking must assimilate these two new frames of reference.

Teilhard de Chardin did not make excessive claim when he wrote:

Blind indeed are those who do not see the sweep of a movement whose orbit infinitely transcends the natural sciences and has successively invaded and conquered the surround-

ing territory—chemistry, physics, sociology and even mathe-
matics and the history of religions. One after the other all
the fields of human knowledge have been shaken and carried away by the same under-water current in the direction
of the study of some *development*. Is evolution a theory, a
system or a hypothesis? It is much more: it is a general condition to which all theories, all hypotheses, all systems must
bow and which they must satisfy henceforward if they are to
be thinkable and true. Evolution is a light illuminating all
facts, a curve that all lines must follow.[1]

I am convinced that our theology of prayer (not to speak
of our Christology) has not yet begun to follow that
curve. Until it does, it will remain for increasing numbers of modern men neither "true" nor any longer even
"thinkable."

Teilhard de Chardin, moreover, has specifically identified for us the man for whom this new perspective has
become compelling:

What makes and classifies a 'modern' man (and a ·vhole host
of our contemporaries is not 'modern' in this sense) is having become capable of seeing in terms not of space and time
alone, but also of duration, or—and it comes to the same
thing—of biological space-time, and above all having become incapable of seeing anything otherwise—anything—
not even himself.[2]

For our purposes here we need add only: *not even himself at prayer!* It is this modern man to whose condition
this book would speak.

One aspect of this perspective of biological space-time

has been developed in the accumulating insight of depth psychology. As Carl Jung puts it:

For more than fifty years we have known, or could have known, that there is an unconscious as a counterbalance to consciousness. Medical psychology has furnished all the necessary empirical and experimental proof of this. There is an unconscious psychic reality which demonstrably influences consciousness and its contents. All this is known, but no practical conclusions have been drawn from it. We still go on thinking and acting as before, as if we were *simplex* and not *duplex*. . . . But actually it is frivolous, superficial and unreasonable of us, as well as psychically unhygienic, to overlook the reaction and standpoint of the unconscious.[3]

We propose to respond to Jung's counsel and to draw some new practical conclusions for the understanding and practice of prayer from this new knowledge which is being so widely disseminated. We shall undertake to see man at prayer as *duplex* rather than merely *simplex*.

Jung points out: "In contrast to the subjectivism of the conscious mind the unconscious is objective, manifesting itself mainly in the form of contrary feelings, fantasies, emotions, impulses and dreams, none of which one makes oneself but which come upon one objectively." [4] He proceeds to suggest: "The religious person, so far as one can judge, stands directly under the influence of the reaction from the unconscious." [5]

Jung raises the crucial question for the modern man we have been describing: "Have I any religious experience and immediate relation to God, and hence that certainty which will keep me, as an individual, from dissolving in the crowd?" [6] Then he expresses the conviction that if the modern man can respond in the affirmative and is willing to fulfill the demands of rigorous self-examination and self-knowledge, "he will have set his hand, as it were, to a declaration of his own human dignity and taken the first steps toward the foundations of his consciousness—that is, toward the unconscious, the only accessible source of religious experience." [7]

We shall be at pains in the chapters that follow to describe this particular modern man who has come habitually to see everything in the perspectives of biological space-time and depth psychology. Thus we see it as our responsibility to carry forward, in these critical areas of the practice of prayer, the insights which Teilhard de Chardin and Carl Jung so effectively presented. For this reason we shall describe and advocate prayer here as itself a phenomenon that must continue to evolve as the most significant aspect of the evolving *phenomenon of man*.

* * *

My gratitude is expressed to Elsie Landstrom, Jane Waller, Douglas Steere, Margaret Lamb, and Flora Symons, all of whom made valuable comments on an earlier version of the present manuscript.

J. R. Y.

To my wife, June,

who has faithfully supported me in my quest, and has helped me to see that prayer should be addressed to the God who has revealed himself in darkness as well as in light.

CONTENTS

CONTENTS

1

ACKNOWLEDGING
THE OBSTACLES TO PRAYER

THERE IS NO religious theme on which communication is as difficult as prayer. Even when the customary reticence is put to one side and we talk to one another about prayer, feelings are often so ambivalent and statements so ambiguous that it becomes difficult to conceal embarrassment. We become aware that we don't really know quite what we feel about prayer, that we haven't thought it through.

On the one hand, when we examine ourselves, we may have to confess that in extremity we do find ourselves praying, on occasion and after a fashion. But we haven't any real confidence in what we are doing, and we have no rationale in support of it. Any sustained practice may long ago have been abandoned, and our sometime praying selves are increasingly out of touch with our other selves. In such a condition, talking with others about prayer is likely to further a sense of separation and alienation rather than to constitute a bond.

Meanwhile, the Church carries on the continuity of its corporate worship, largely propelled, one suspects, by the incredible momentum of more than three thousand years of the Judaeo-Christian heritage. The liturgy is rehearsed and the sonorous cadences of the prayers intoned. But to more and more reflective persons the practice seems like a vain incantation because they are not convinced of the meaning and value of prayer itself. The churches would be out of business if corporate worship were to be abandoned. At the same time, while it isn't the kind of statistic the Gallup Poll could effectively gather for us, one has the impression that private prayer may well be in a state of advanced decay. We must ask the inevitable question: Can corporate worship retain any vitality if the participants cease to pray faithfully in private?

The Decline of Prayer

On this critical issue the Church appears to maintain a conspiracy of silence. If prayer is the lifeblood of the Church, as earlier centuries maintained, is not this vital stream now suffering from severe anemia? Insofar as individual pastors and rabbis have been worthy of the title "man of God" rather than "man of the cloth" or "ecclesiastical organization man," one instinctively knows that the unmistakable marks of authenticity have been tempered in the white heat of solitary prayer.

The decline in private prayer is not characteristic of the congregation alone; many priests and pastors no longer pray in private as was once their custom. And has not this disparity between what is publicly encouraged, at least in part to keep the institution going, and privately neglected for whatever reason, produced the most dangerous credibility gap the Church has ever suffered? Can even the prophetic utterances, in which the Church does seem more genuinely prolific today than for some years past, continue to win respect if priests and pastors become progressively severed from the source of renewal in solitary communion? P. T. Forsyth has reminded us that private prayer can be, and often is, more truly common prayer than some forms of public worship.

The vast response a few years ago to the first book by John Robinson, when Bishop of Woolwich, was in part an expression of gratitude for his having restored for the moment, as one of its respected bishops, a spirit of credibility toward the Church. The commendable attempt to be "honest to God" amid so much of the Church's dishonesty toward man was profoundly appreciated by many laymen who had too long experienced a cavalier brush-off by clergy when they reported their searching and frustrations with the private practice of prayer. A deep sense of solidarity between clergy and laity was established, at least temporarily, when the Bishop made the public confession of the near bankruptcy of his own private prayer. Many were moved by this breakthrough of communication by simple honesty where they no longer thought to look for it.

No doubt many consciences were also relieved when John Robinson further confided that he had made some measure of peace with himself by acknowledging his failures in prayer and no longer felt as guilty about them. But despite the Bishop's admirable and refreshing honesty, nothing was offered that would hearten the seeker who wanted to find the way forward into vital prayer instead of merely assuaging his conscience in its abandonment. Again, P. T. Forsyth is helpful in suggesting that the worst sin is prayerlessness, and the only death is not to want to pray any more. Anyone in whose experience this word has the ring of reality cannot draw comfort from the Bishop's statement. Once the disarming confession has been made, and men have acknowledged that it reflects a prevailing condition in the Church, the real task is to construct a credible and persuasive rationale for prayer. Modern man is, on the whole, not quite prepared to forfeit what he dimly realizes might be the benefits of prayer, if he could be helped to resume the practice with renewed passion.

I am speaking to that man who, despite continued doubt and long neglect, is unable to accept the counsel that he should no longer feel guilty for not praying. He suspects that the whole household of faith might fall if prayer in solitude were to cease once and for all. He also suspects, because no one has ever convinced him to the contrary, that if he personally stops praying or perhaps never brings himself really to begin, he may lose forever his chance to be the self he had it in him, with

4

the help of prayer, to become. This man cannot be reconciled to his own state of prayerlessness.

Traditional Obstacles to Prayer

There have always been formidable obstacles to prayer. Some of these have been philosophical problems about the existence of any god to whom prayer might be addressed. There were agnostics and atheists among the ancients, and they have never wanted for successors. For a time the Church attempted to marshal logical proofs of the existence of God, but the skeptic has always been adept at raising one more ultimate question, challenging one more unexamined premise. In addition, man has repeatedly posed questions as to how God could be both all-powerful and all-loving at the same time. And always there has been the insistent question arising from personal experience which Job first articulated for us: Why is it that the evil so often prosper and the good suffer? Elie Wiesel tells us, in his novel *Night,* that he knows the exact moment when God died for him: the moment when he saw the flames and smoke arising from the gas chambers of Auschwitz where his mother and sister had been killed.

Other obstacles to prayer arise from internal moral duplicity. Every perceptive counselor for centuries has recognized that individuals may profess intellectual doubt when the real problem is inner moral conflict. If I am unwilling to release a long-held hatred, shall I not hesitate to come into the presence of the One who I know would demand this of me? If I am unwilling or unable to relinquish or to transform a relationship which gives the lie to another relationship, even if I am the only witness, how shall I bring myself to commune with the One to whom, I have been taught from infancy, "all thoughts are open, all desires known, and from whom no secrets are hid"? True prayer would require of me a purging I cannot perform. Unconsciously I am driven to rationalize that I no longer believe in prayer. Further, prayer in solitude is hard work and calls for a degree of self-discipline I may be unwilling to undertake. Laziness and lethargy as well as preoccupation may also stand in my way.

New Obstacles to Prayer

The Evolutionary Perspective: Thus far the obstacles are ancient as well as modern, but modern man has additional intellectual problems which give him pause. These arise from two perspectives to which he has only recently become heir: the evolutionary and the depth-psychological. Both have confronted him with new questions concerning the meaning and value of prayer.

Modern man is post-Darwinian. Ever since the discovery of the fact of the evolutionary process, nothing relating to man can ever look quite the same again to one who sees what is involved. Julian Huxley has insisted that this new knowledge about himself is the greatest self-disclosure in man's entire history. It has enabled him to place himself, as it were, in space and time. In man, evolution has become conscious of itself for the first time. Teilhard de Chardin described the modern man as one who can no longer see anything, including himself, save in terms of biological space-time or duration.

For himself, Teilhard worked out a great synthesis which bound into one his two worlds of science and theology; but other minds have boggled before the new questions which this perspective has leveled upon faith, and upon prayer in particular. Later, in the progression of our thought, we shall attempt to relate our interpretation of prayer to this new perspective. For the present, we want simply to identify some of the new obstacles to prayer that have been raised by this pervasive frame of reference.

We have had to adjust our thinking to make way for a continuing creation rather than a completed one. There are clearly new beings as well as new things under the sun, not to speak of what may be happening under other suns. This truth, after some initial shock, we might have been able to encompass had we found compelling evidence that the Creator, still at work in the evolutionary process, was readily identifiable as the Judaeo-Christian God. But there have been observable characteristics in the process which are not easily harmonized with our preconceptions of the traditional Deity.

There is the extravagant waste, for one thing. A God whose attention is fixed upon the falling of a single sparrow and who numbers the hairs of our heads, is hard to reconcile with one who experiments endlessly with new variations of species and is quite prepared to assign to extinction those that do not succeed in ad-

7

justing effectively to their environment. If over-specialization spells their doom, who but their Maker can be blamed for implanting the seed of such ultimate disaster?

Confronted by a nature known always in some of its aspects as red in tooth and claw, it was once possible to suggest plausibly that some restructuring was necessary, as with the redemption of man, but that ultimately the lion could be expected to lie down with the lamb. However, our current ecological vision of the total interdependence and interpenetration of everything within a given environment has converted what might have been interpreted as an accidental aberration, due to some mythical fall, into a picture of survival portraying one form of life preying ceaselessly upon others.

What kind of deity must we hold responsible for so shaping the patterns of life and death? Arguments supporting an amoral and fortuitous contingency, instead of an intelligent and moral planning, would seem to flow more readily from the new facts presented by our altered perspective. How, indeed, can one discern a supreme being, identifiable with the Judaeo-Christian God, behind this process with which, as Teilhard suggests, all other processes must come to terms? If one can conceive of an *author* and *sustainer* of such unceasing experimentation, how and in what spirit does one go about addressing him in prayer?

The Depth-Psychological Perspective: Moreover, if we are post-Darwinian, we are also post-Freudian. The unbroken continuity of life on this planet, which makes us in a real sense as old as the process itself, is discovered to have inward dimensions as well as outward manifestations in changing shapes and capabilities with respect to the ecological environment. Mechanistic interpretations of cause and effect are equally applicable to the psychological operations of man's inner world. In erecting the theory of the unconscious and the laws which make it function as it does, Freud left no room for the objective reality of the Judaeo-Christian God. By implication, he subjected prayer to scrutiny as a phenomenon attributable to illusion, arising from man's unconscious psychological needs. The image of God has emerged, he suggests, from the projections upon a posited person who is supposed to be the source and sustainer of the universe, of one's need to perpetuate certain tender and comforting feelings fostered in childhood by a protective and loving father. In a similar way the impulse to pray, one would gather, must be understood as no more than a psychological need to continue in the present the interior sense of dependence and security experienced as a child within the sphere of the father's love. Prayer, therefore, is made to appear childish and its continued practice an evidence of immaturity.

Our condition is even worse. A knowledge of the mechanistic inner workings of this abysmal world of the unconscious reveals that all motivations are suspect, even the subject matter of our prayers. All can be explained in terms of early experiences and their debilitating perpetuation in the unconscious. Conscience, and the moral guidance whose voice we imagined to be that of the Holy Spirit, is but the accumulated implantation of taboos and sanctions imposed by a culture upon its children. Sin and guilt can be understood as culture-related, and therefore relative rather than absolute.

Noble aspirations have their less commendable underpinnings in mechanized causation related to the need for approval and acceptance, involving of course self-approval and self-acceptance as well. Man's unconscious creation of a God to whom he can speak words of praise and adoration, and to whom he can give thanks, is, we are told, a psychological necessity for a being who, as he grows out of the protective environment of his childhood, has to offset an intolerable loneliness by "peopling" it with a just and tender and loving God with whom he can carry on the comforting but nevertheless illusory converse of prayer.

Thus, in addition to the obstacles to prayer that modern man shares with his predecessors, there is not only the disconcerting knowledge that his life and being have arisen within the context of the evolutionary process, but also the nagging suspicion that the need to pray originates in psychological illusion and that its pursuit is a form of weakness and immaturity. Even if, in spite of all that modern depth-psychological insights have revealed to him about himself, a man persists in the conviction that there remains a realm within for a divine presence, how shall he set about disentangling the voice of that presence from the voices of long-repressed desires and resulting transferences, identifications, and projections? In the maze of the unconscious presented to him by his dreams and waking fantasies, how shall he find his way back into any confidence in prayer?

Add to this the influence of positivist philosophical thought of our time, which teaches man to acknowledge as real only that to which his physical senses can respond, only that which can be measured by them on some scale. What I cannot see, touch, taste, feel, or smell has no existence in reality. To what realm are notions of the existence of God thereby relegated? Add further, an extension of the point of view expressed in Harvey Cox's *The Secular City* of the progressive shrinkage in God's domain as man's knowledge increases. As modern medicine has largely replaced man's dependence upon faith-healing, as astrophysics takes the place of earlier cosmologies, are there new practices or sciences that now make prayer anachronistic?

If there have always been obstacles to the practice of prayer, how enormously multiplied they have become to modern man. Is it any wonder that with reference to prayer, as the practice has been classically understood, modern man should now feel as though he were lost in an impenetrable and alien forest, a child crying in the night for a home and a voice he suspects may never have existed?

2

ESTABLISHING THE
GROUND FOR CONFIDENCE

THE DESOLATE FEELING of being lost in the woods is not modern. As we have seen, however, there are some peculiarly modern dimensions to this experience. Men of earlier centuries were not confronted by the realization that they were involved in an evolutionary process producing creatures who failed, as well as others who succeeded, in adapting to their environment. No previous generation, moreover, has been confronted by the discoveries of depth psychology which call into question the validity and values of our motivations and aspirations.

If an earlier generation was tempted to believe in a philosophy of inevitable progress, ours can amass considerable evidence to the contrary. It is understandable that the cult of the Absurd should draw its devotees from those who feel that in all honesty every potentially false reassurance should be abandoned. They would appear to argue for a reversal of the biblical movement from chaos to order as if the notion of this movement were itself the original illusion. Are we, then, perhaps returning, as the novels and plays of Samuel Beckett seem to imply, to a state of being, without form and devoid of meaning?

The Recurring Sense of Presence

Though modern man's anxiety has a new pitch of intensity, arising from the unanswered questions prompted by his expanding knowledge and experience of himself, the source of reassurance remains what it has always been—the ever-recurring sense of a presence. As the light of the sun penetrates the densest woods and falls intermittently upon the undergrowth, illuminating the darkness for a short while, the light of this presence, however generally eclipsed by our preoccupations, aberrations, and depressions, continues to reassure us that we have not altogether lost our way.

Primitive man senses a presence in sun and moon, mountains and valleys, trees and rivers, rocks and soil. More sophisticated man progressively disengages specific presence from objects in nature, but he persists in positing a supreme being, essentially formless and imageless, yet occasionally diaphanous in the sense of shining through matter. Whether we call this presence God, Brahma, the Absolute, the Self, we must acknowledge in our quest for the basis of prayer that this universal and immemorial experience of the Supreme Being has its source in man himself. It arises out of the interior experience of individual men in their encounter with something or someone in themselves and in other men.

This realization is central to our argument in support of prayer. We have fallen into the habit of assuming that the Church's authority for propagating the idea of the existence of God rests upon other, more conclusive evidence. This is not the case. No one has ever had access to any objective evidence not available to each one of us today. When this simple fact has come home to us, we may find our faith shaken for a time. But intimations of real presence continue to reappear in the only place men have ever known them, in themselves and in their fellows, living and dead. So, while our first reaction may be one of distrust at having been deceived by the Church on this matter, a new confidence emerges from the realization that we can experience and judge for ourselves the only evidence anyone has ever had.

It may be appalling at first to see that the whole structure of faith in the existence and nature of God, and in response through prayer, hangs upon this single thread of experience. But it is better that we acknowledge this fact at the outset than expose ourselves to deeper disillusionment later in the pursuit of prayer on the basis of any false premises. Let me state it again: Man's notion of the being and attributes of God is ultimately dependent solely upon his experience of a presence in himself, not altogether himself, and of a presence in other men, not to be wholly identified with themselves.

Once this mysterious presence is given a name, and some of his attributes and qualities identified, one may experience his reflection in other aspects of nature, but the initial awareness of this being we call God came to man in encounter with something or someone in himself and in other men. To be sure, characteristically, he immediately projected this sense of presence upon whatever created and sustains the universe. There is certainly some truth in Freud's contention that man projects upon a hypothetical Father in heaven the inward image of a peculiarly tender, selfless, and altruistic love some men have experienced at the hands of their human fathers. We know very little of Joseph the carpenter. But that his son, Jesus of Nazareth, should so naturally have addressed his heavenly Father in prayer tells us all we need to know about Joseph.

We must also honestly confess to ourselves and to each other that since we are dealing with what is still completely shrouded in mystery, namely the ultimate source and end of what we call personality, we may indeed be mistaken. The existence and nature of God as we now conceive him may in the future turn out to be an unjustifiable projection. But any such conclusive dénouement would appear to be a long way ahead. We know nothing of the beginning or the end of the universe in the way we know something of the evolution of our planet since its birth. All is conjecture. What we do know is that we do experience intimations of the existence in ourselves of an *other,* not wholly ourselves, and in our fellows, distinguishable from themselves. We have nothing more on which to base this preposterous hope. But there it is, and despite all our current conditioning in favor of rejecting the evidence as illusory, we persist in experiencing this presence and are drawn to respond in prayer.

The Sense of Presence in Ourselves

In ourselves this presence makes himself known in a number of ways. We know ourselves to be at once far worse and far better than the nearest person to us ever dreams. We should not know how to confess the worst of our waking imaginings and impulses, not to speak of our dreams. We may be inclined to attribute their source and the autonomous complexes that develop around them to possession by the Devil, or some other personification of the demonic. But we also sometimes experience great good in ourselves, or rather someone good in ourselves. We are aware that this someone evokes from us a sense of awe and wonder, the numinous, the holy. It is as if our surface self, the persistent identity preserved miraculously in our stream of consciousness, were, almost in spite of itself, now and again in dialogue with this other. Though we remain hopelessly ambivalent, we can see what we are doing from his point of view. He stands in judgment on us, but is at the same time compassionate and forgiving. He restores us to communion with himself. It is unthinkable that he should ever excommunicate us, though we find that we sometimes deliberately excommunicate ourselves for a season because we pursue a course of action or thought in which a concurrent sense of his presence and of our betrayal of him would be too painful for us.

Some take the view that this is clearly the voice of conscience, shaped by social sanctions and taboos. But that theory does not adequately account for the sense of the presence we experience of a person who makes his home in the depths of our being. We sometimes feel he knows something about us we do not know ourselves. He can reveal to us the truth about ourselves. If we are obedient to his promptings, no matter how lonely and difficult the road, we are rewarded by a sense of his more sustained presence and companionship. When we deliberately disregard the demands of the relationship, the sense of presence fades. As long as we know that he is still there, we can respect ourselves, even profoundly love ourselves, because our companion gratuitously makes his home in us. We live with him under the same roof. There are moments when we are so close that the dialogue becomes wordless, idea-less communion, and, once in a long while, an experience of union and identification.

Acquainted with some of the findings of modern depth psychology, we are naturally wary lest we suffer, in this impression, some kind of schizophrenia, a double or multiple split in our own psyche. But if this experience were the result of such sickness, it would manifest itself in disunion, dissociation, incoherence, and erratic behavior. Yet when we cultivate this interior relationship with some discipline we find we move in the direction of greater wholeness and integration and are capable of more consistent, compassionate, and effective living.

The Sense of Presence in Other Men

Our consciousness of this presence within ourselves is affected by what others in our Western religious tradition have said about the attributes of God. It is also affected by our direct experience of this same being in other persons. Sometimes we are able to distinguish between the person of someone we know and this being who makes himself known to us through that other person. We catch a glimpse of his beauty and holiness, his resourcefulness in compassion and love, speaking to us through a friend. T. S. Eliot has beautifully expressed this elusive but common human experience in lines that seem to allude to the Easter experience of the two on the road to Emmaus in the Gospel of St. Luke:

Who is the third who walks always beside you?
When I count there are only you and I together
But when I look ahead up the white road
There is always another walking beside you
Gliding wrapt in a brown mantle, hooded,
I do not know whether a man or a woman—
But who is that on the other side of you? [1]

Just as we are able to distinguish when a friend is not himself but is carried away by some mood or temper not unlike a "possession," so we know when we can see past him to another on the other side of him, or in him, who is better than our friend knows how to be.

It was the good fortune of the disciples to meet this other in Jesus of Nazareth. It is true that they brought to this human encounter preconceived ideas of the nature of God and the fixed conviction that he would send at some point his Messiah to usher in his kingdom. The identification of this figure with Jesus gradually took place in their minds. But they were first drawn to a person who exercised for them a strange fascination, who seemed to understand them better than they understood themselves, and who possessed an uncanny wisdom about life. They found they were prepared to trust this man whom they first called Rabbi, and only later, "My Lord and my God."

The process of identification was furthered by an Easter experience of resurrection, however one may understand what happened that day, and by a Pentecost experience of new power flowing through them and binding them together. It was continued in Paul's creation of the cosmic dimensions of Christ and in John's doctrine of his pre-existence as logos. The end of this process is not yet. But the original experience of the disciples, I believe, should be understood in terms of seeing the divine being just the other side of Jesus, or as dwelling in Jesus, and as making demands upon them which they could neither ignore nor escape.

I would hold the view that the difference between Jesus and them, as well as between Jesus and ourselves, is not one of kind but of degree. Jesus had so sustained his own interior dialogue with this being he characteristically called Father, and so committed himself to the will of this Father, that the disciples came to the ultimate identification of his person with the divine will and being in the notion of Father and Son. But for our purpose in wanting to learn how to pray, our approach to him should be as disciples to teacher or rabbi, so that we may come to understand how he related to this being in himself, in others, and in nature. Fortunately we have a portrait of Jesus in the Gospel stories which, however wanting in detail, enables us also to see the other just beyond and in him as we of the Christian religion have seen him in no other man.

Alan Watts has put forward the interesting idea, arising no doubt from a cross-fertilization of Zen Buddhist and Christian thought, that the one God who dwells within the being of each one of us is like an actor who has so identified with the role he is playing that he has forgotten who he is. God recollects who he is in this drama only when individual men, notably the mystics, come to know whose they are and who he is who dwells within them and with whom they feel at one. To many Christians this notion may seem heresy. Yet it is one way to account by metaphor for the experience so many have of the interior presence and of identification between this presence and the counterpart in other men. George Fox counseled men to "walk cheerfully over the earth, answering to that of God in everyman." It is only God in us who can recognize and answer to that of God in others. We are also obliged to respond to that of God in ourselves.

The Impulse to Respond

If there is not this being seeking us from within ourselves and other men, then we know nothing of the existence of God, and any attempt to respond to him in prayer is absurd. On the other hand, as long as we are moved by this immediate sense of presence, and until we can be persuaded that we are self-deceived, there persists the haunting fear that not to respond to *the* person as to a person is to jeopardize our own great opportunity to become and to remain ourselves, our best potential selves. For, even on the human level of friendship, are we not, in part, created by our friends? My mother gave me physical birth. But she is only one of those, not necessarily the most important, who gave birth in me to various aspects of my own potential. She and my father were in some sense responsible for the peculiar combination of genes that went into my formation. But I cannot credit my parents with the accumulated potential in the unbroken succession of genes going back to my animal, amphibian, and fish forebears —not to mention the mysterious potential that lay asleep in matter until life began on this planet.

There has been a succession of individuals, some of whom are remembered and cherished in a golden thread of the continuity of confirmation I secretly acknowledge, others whom I have forgotten or never recognized. But I owe to these what Eckhart called the noble birth of the life of the soul in me quite as much as I owe to my parents my physical birth and initial potential and limitations. These friends of my spirit had the wisdom and the insight to perceive in me talents and qualities that might never have developed, but for them. In an extraordinarily sure-footed way in her book titled *Creative Prayer,* Mrs. Herman describes the process for us:

As we are initiated into the mystery of friendship, we know that our friend is not merely "another"; he speaks to us not from without, but from the center of our being. He is in us and we in him. His influence is profoundly mystical; no merely temperamental affinity can account for friendship at its highest potency. Deep down in the abysmal mystery of being was the thread spun that linked soul to soul. My friend creates me and recreates me. In him I come to know my true self. His love and trust purge me of sin by shame and contrition; his gentleness makes me great; his high expectations make all things possible to me.[2]

If this is true of human friendship at its best, what might not be possible for relationship to the divine friend? If a human friend can in some sense create and recreate me, what might not God do for me if I were to be as attentive to him? But all will depend upon my readiness to cultivate this relationship in prayer. This will require time and effort and patience. When I am with my friend I know that he is there. When I go into my room and close the door to be alone with God, the evidence of his presence is less compelling. It is a matter sometimes of hope against despair, of faith against doubt. I believe, and cry for help because of my unbelief. When I believe in my friend, the will is at rest. With God I must sometimes will to believe. At times the attempt to meet God in prayer will seem perilously close to make-believe. At other times his presence is as real to me as I am to myself, and I am passionately aware that only here am I truly known, only here truly myself. I am surprised by joy and invaded by peace as long as this strong sense of presence remains.

The Projection of Presence on the Universe

Once again, the whole venture of prayer is ultimately based upon the scientifically nonverifiable experience which many men have had of a divine presence within themselves and other men. From this experience, and confirmation by the witness of others, attributes of God were identified and recorded by the authors of the Bible. There is remarkable concurrence in the scriptures of the other living religions. There can also be transference and projection of the sense of the same presence upon nature or upon individual aspects of, or objects in, nature. Wordsworth can report with candor and passion:

> And I have felt
> A presence that disturbs me with the joy
> Of elevated thoughts; a sense sublime
> Of something far more deeply interfused,
> Whose dwelling is the light of setting suns,
> And the round ocean and the living air,
> And the blue sky, and in the mind of man:
> A motion and a spirit, that impels
> All thinking things, all objects of all thought,
> And rolls through all things.[3]

But had not this sense been encountered first "in the mind of man," it could not have been transferred to "the light of setting suns, the round ocean, the living air, and the blue sky." Flowers, mountains, valleys, sunsets might have struck men as aesthetically satisfying. Man might have arrived at a sense of relatedness to them, of belongingness with them. But insofar as they speak to him of the God of compassion and mercy, this is clearly a projection from man's original knowledge and acquaintance with this God in himself and in his fellow man. Perhaps some such recognition lies behind the penetrating and curiously modern words of William Blake:

> Thou Art a Man, God is no more,
> Thine own Humanity learn to Adore.[4]

In the phrase "God is no more" some might hope to find support for a "death of God" theology. But surely Blake is rather implying that all we know of God has come to us through man himself. This is ample support for the most optimistic humanism. What we adore in God is something that has presented itself to our consciousness first and foremost in man. But of course we know, and Blake knew, that the God man conceives, if he be at all, is more than man. His goodness is greater than any man has ever achieved. Jesus insisted that no man should call him good, for there is only one who is good, and that one is God. As no one is as good as the God that man can imagine, so no society has ever yet embodied the corporate good that men can contemplate as the Kingdom of God. Until man is good and the Kingdom is here, we are to adore something in our own humanity from which alone this vision miraculously springs.

Finally, as we note that God in a profound sense can be no more for man than man at his best has envisioned him, so we must confess that the individual man's God can only be what that man, in the present stage of his own development, insight, and imagination, can conceive. If the great conjecture turn out to be basically true, every man's present God will be revealed as too small. But no man's God need remain small. Every man's God will be different from every other man's God. This is the leap of valid insight, perhaps unconscious, behind Genesis' recognition of the existence of the God of Abraham, the God of Isaac, and the God of Jacob. All forms of prayer are ways of relating to one's own God as to the person whose presence first aroused in man the irresistible need to respond in prayer. If one does respond and remain without ceasing in dialogue with his God, his knowledge of God grows and expands, and he finds himself gradually transformed by the interior relationship.

William James called prayer "intercourse with an ideal companion." Psychologically this is a perceptive description. There can be no convincing response to the skeptic's whisper that the companion may be the creation of the unconscious to assuage the intolerable loneliness of human life. But the pragmatist is able to observe a difference in quality of life between him who abandons prayer as illusion and him who, knowing the risk he takes, wills to believe. And what if this ideal companion were discovered to be the new man taking shadowy shape, with all the patience of evolution, in contemporary man? Would not this but further confirm the notion that the purposeful finger of the creator had not yet been withdrawn from the shaping of the new Adam?

3

ASSIMILATING PRAYER
IN OUR WORLD VIEW

PRAYER IS MAN'S instinctive response to the immediate experience of the *other* within. It is a phenomenon arising from his compelling need to relate to this being who seeks him out, makes ultimate demands, but also forgives, accepts, and offers help. Given all our reservations and hesitations about the validity of prayer, together with, at the same time, this persistent experience of presence, the mind is forced, in the interest of unity and wholeness, to construct a world view that makes a plausible place for prayer.

Is not the distinctive function of religion, by derivation of the word, to bind everything into one bundle? While reason lacks the capacity to prove the reality of the presence, neither can the mind effectively summon reason to disprove it. Recognizing the possibility of illusion, the mind is required to conceive a model in which the experience of the presence to whom prayer is addressed can be harmonized with the new evolutionary and depth-psychological perspectives with which modern man must cope. The will cannot be expected to carry forward a disciplined practice that reason cannot accept, at least experimentally.

The Immanence of God

While we can no longer imagine any place "out there" in space where a transcendent God can make his home, there is the alternative possibility that this person-like being indwells all of creation, that he is, indeed, in some sense, "in here." We have the testimony of the mystics that in their experience he is nearer than the extremities of their own bodies, nearer than breath itself. This does not mean that God is to be identified outright with everything. He is rather to be recognized as a diaphanous presence within the rest of nature as well as in man. Teilhard makes extraordinary confession of the nature of his own recurring mystical experience:

Throughout my life, by means of my life, the world has little by little caught fire in my sight until, aflame all around me, it has become almost completely luminous from within. . . . such has been my experience in contact with the earth—the diaphany of the Divine at the heart of the universe on fire—Christ; His heart; a fire: capable of penetrating everywhere and gradually spreading everywhere.[1]

For Teilhard the presence is identified as Christ. For others of us the name of the one who thus addresses us from within the core of his still evolving universe is God, or the Holy Spirit; for still others, Brahma or the Absolute. For Teilhard's "modern man," who professes no specific religious faith, the mysterious presence may represent aspects of the being man has it in him to become.

We know nothing of how the universe began, and we can know nothing of how it will end, if indeed we can say it *began* at all or will have an end. But we are aware of a particular value expressing itself in what we call personality, itself an indescribable mystery. We have no knowledge that personality exists anywhere in the universe outside of man. We are aware that it is anthropomorphic of us to feel that this value which we find in man is the greatest in the universe. Yet we are men, and cannot see ourselves from any other point of view than that of men.

We can let the imagination play on what we must seem like to other animate beings who respond in one way or another to us. Why does my dog so persistently seek my attention and affection? Once, in a game preserve in Africa, a giraffe lowered his head to peer at me with soft, velvety eyes through the window of my car. Did his curious, wistful gaze speak of a momentary impulse to relate to me in the shared world of all living things? But there is a great gulf fixed between us. We do not know how to communicate with each other.

On the other hand, as Carl Jung reminds us in his autobiography,[2] there are times when we are not sure of the exact borders of things, of the place where our skin-encapsulated bodies end and the boundaries of other objects begin. There is in those moments the impression that we are part of a total organism, all of it somehow alive, and all of it interrelated and interdependent, as is every part of our own bodies. At other times, the impression may be more accurately described as the feeling that there is something alive in us that is also alive in everything about us, and that whatever happens to our being at death, this other cannot know death. This mystical consciousness may be the evolving, emerging faculty in man, to be valued above all else. While we know that we have these experiences, we do not know their meaning in relation to the rest of the universe in the present, past, or future.

The Origin of Life

We do know now that there was a time on this earth when there was no life at all. We know that the bodies of living beings are made up of the same chemical elements that are to be found in inanimate objects. We know that at a given time in the evolution of this planet the molecular structures of these elements were transformed miraculously into cellular substance. We know that this transformation has not yet taken place within the life of the one other orbiting body of which we have a first-hand experience, the moon. We can observe that the environmental factors which support life on this planet, in terms of temperature, atmosphere, presence of water and vegetation, are missing on the moon. Even those virus forms which are increasingly thought to be the most primitive life are lacking. On the other hand, we are told by scientists that probability favors the existence of life on some planets in other solar systems.

We know that once life began on the earth, whether vegetable or animal, a process of reproduction was simultaneously initiated, and that all that is living now is in direct descent from the as yet unaccountable emergence of life at that particular period in the earth's history. Since then, even on this planet, which possesses, for all we know, the only living beings in the universe, nothing has sprung into life from inanimate being. There is only the transference of life through reproduction. We are driven to the inference that matter itself, at least some matter, has contained from time immemorial the seed of life, awaiting certain exterior environmental conditions to draw it forth.

We know that new species have evolved as a result of the interaction between the inherent potential of existing species and the ever-changing environment of which they are a part. Darwin names this process which accounts for the origin of species "natural selection." It has appeared to some to involve what has been called "random adaptation" because the interaction between interior potential and exterior conditioning seems fortuitous. There are, however, certain factors which remain constant, rules of the game as it were, which hold despite the almost infinite range of possibilities for surprise in outcome. It is, indeed, an "unexpected universe" as Loren Eiseley calls it in the title of one of his books.[3] Nevertheless, a study of the process of evolution does lead us to expect the continuation of what we may look upon as certain criteria of advance.

Once the general patterns of bodily structure have been established, further development must take place within that framework. Even when species revert to earlier habitats and life-styles, as when some mammals, which had evolved for some time on land, return to the sea, they retain recognizable continuity in physiological structure and function. Animals do not return to earlier evolutionary forms of their forebears, and once a species has become extinct it is not reproduced by any currently evolving species. In this sense evolution is irreversible.

Development and Adaptation

Moreover, within the process progress may be measured by the phenomenon Teilhard named "complexification." That is to say, as creatures evolve they become more complex. At the same time the ground rules require that as complexification takes place a corresponding unification must also take place, so that the new adaptations and consequent functions are integrated with all the other characteristics and potentials in the creature. Thus there is even more remarkable unity in the presence of increasing complexity. The present summit has been realized in man. The human being, in bodily structure and in the mature individuation of personality, is at once the most complex and, at the same time, the most highly integrated creature of all.

One knows his friend despite that friend's fluctuating moods and interests under varying circumstances. If he is a "man of parts," the unity and integrity of the wholeness are the more valued. That man is most admired of whom it might be said that he is "a man for all seasons," meaning that no matter how much circumstances and conditions about him may change, nor how sensitive he is to the change in all about him, he can be counted on to remain the same in his interior commitments and consistent in his behavior. We could even say of him, "the more he (as well as all about him) changes the more he remains the same."

We learn also that, in addition to interior harmony, there must be harmony and balance in the relationship of a species to everything in the environment. Constant change in environment demands continuing adaptability. If an animal overspecializes in response to one aspect of the environment in such a way as to limit his adaptability to new conditions, he may be doomed to extinction, as happened in the case of the dinosaurs and the saber-toothed tigers, for example. Bodily adaptations to one set of environmental conditions limited adequate flexibility of response to new conditions. This principle also applies to cultures within the human species. Those cultures have survived and continued to evolve which were capable of responding creatively to changing environment, whether occasioned by ecological factors or the impact of another culture or both.

When we reflect upon man's present condition, one

of the critical questions is whether or not he is engaging in forms of specialization that may spell his own extinction as a species: for example, his technological preoccupations. He has now created weapons which are intended for use in the extension or defense of national interests and ideological concepts. At present, according to the philosophy of balance of power, lethal weapons, from the point of view of the preservation of the species, are manufactured and stock-piled only for the sake of deterrence. But they cannot serve effectively within this diabolical context as deterrents unless, at the same time, their possible use remains credible to the enemy. In the meantime, there is always the possibility of a vast conflagration being touched off by accident, misinterpretation, or miscalculation, even if none of the great powers is mad enough willfully to initiate another world war. If that should happen, the species will, in effect, commit suicide.

This is the major threat to the survival of mankind, but it is not the only one. Technology has been developed and pursued thus far by man in the production of goods in almost total disregard of the effect either upon social institutions or upon an ecological balance in the environment favorable to the health and well-being of man. The advance of technology, in the context of given economic, social, and political institutions, has aggravated some problems and created new ones which threaten the disintegration of society unless radical social change comes swiftly enough. At the same time man's uncontrolled technological development, taken together with population expansion and the phenomenon of urbanization, has produced a degree of pollution in water and air and soil that also threatens his extinction. And while we rejoice that modern medicine has been able to reduce infant mortality and to extend life expectancy, unless the species has the wisdom, now, voluntarily to limit its reproduction, it may become too numerous to be supported by the heretofore "good" earth.

Reflecting on the past, we cannot deny the extravagant waste which the evolutionary process has strewn over the surface of the earth. The evidence in the earth's strata is incontrovertible, and even a cursory glance at the present living representatives of the unending chain of development conveys the same impression. Why should the author of a process so marvelous in some of its products be responsible for so many failures and so much lost motion? Why could not the process have been more selective all along and moved more surely and swiftly to such an admirable being as man at his best? From one point of view all would seem contingency rather than purposeful advance toward a preconceived objective. A human engineer experiments and often fails too, but his failures do not live and breathe and destroy each other in an unending interaction in the struggle to survive. These questions give pause to a glib optimism, and remain still unanswered.

Purpose and Direction

But if we question whether man himself represents one line of advance from the initiation of the process we have but to imagine a film, recording this advance, run backward on the screen. The achievements of community and corporate research, great masterpieces of art and the sensibilities which produce them, the skillful and compassionate human care of human beings, these are among the first to fade into their earlier undeveloped beginnings. Tribal warfare, head-hunting, cannibalism return. One looks in vain for the "noble savage." A little later the forebears of man drop from the erect posture to all fours and spend more time in the trees than on the ground, with notable accompanying loss of the adept use of the forelegs and paws, and the shrinkage in the size as well as the capacity of the brain. Then the amphibian line emerges and the backward recession is drawn as by an irresistible suction to the first mother, the sea. Finally, life is reabsorbed in inanimate matter. We may doubt any objective purpose in our more discouraging moments, but to contemplate the process in reverse is to be compelled to acknowledge that we are the product of some *direction* and that this direction has been, in some reassuring sense, forward.

Up through the entire tree of life there has surged, through these eons of time, the sap of consciousness. Moreover, consciousness itself evolves. In man it has reached the highest point yet attained on this planet. If the particular form of consciousness which we designate the mystical—that is, the consciousness of undifferentiated unity involving interior identification with other persons and other things in nature and with nature's author—is the growing edge of consciousness in man, the authentic mystics would then be the "sports" of the species, the forerunners of the new man, the man to be, the "Son of man." Moreover, have not the mystics always known experimentally the interpenetration and interdependence to which the science of ecology has begun to testify?

Some men have a curious capacity to conceive in imagination a Kingdom of God upon earth, and to begin now to live as if that Kingdom were realized. Their interior commitments were made, not in conformity with the things of this world as they now are, but with this envisioned community which has existed only in the minds of saints and seers. Yet that ideal realm has become for them more real than the actual world about them. It has won their allegiance; their true citizenship is there. Consequently, hidden within their being is a fulcrum capable of exerting leverage on the whole species, moving it an infinitesimal degree toward the new man.

Teilhard argues that the *alpha* of the entire process, from the beginning of being, not just living beings, has been God, and that the *omega* is the Christification of the universe, an end of the times (*eschaton*), in which Christ will have returned and will reign supreme, in which all being, animate and inanimate, will alike reflect freely willed and happy obedience and harmony. All that the Hallelujah Chorus presages will have been fulfilled. Appealing as this vision is, I do not believe that we are justified in fixing any particular image. We are as little qualified to do so as were our animal forebears to contemplate what it would be like to be a good man in a world in which there were as yet no men.

But if we cannot know the end of man, nor predict with any ultimate assurance an omega point, we have at least become aware of direction; and religious men do have a measure of consensus as to what the new man will be like. We cannot conceive the distant future, nor even the near future of ten thousand years hence. But we do have a vision of what would constitute a relatively good society several hundred years from now. We know a good deal about the direction in which man has moved in his ascent from the sea, and we know in what direction he must move if he would survive and build the good society. It is clear that he must abandon any tribal, racial, or class bigotry, and begin to "build the earth."

Man must reclaim his environment from the pollution for which he is himself responsible. No other animal has ever so fouled his own nest. Building the earth requires not only purifying the environment but creating a form of world government and shaping institutions that make for peace, for the compassionate care of all who suffer, and for the advancement of knowledge. As the world becomes one community in which population is controlled, cooperation replaces competition, and the only relevant politics becomes the politics of ecology, we shall need to learn how to retain individuality and diversity in spite of inevitable collectivism. So, while we cannot know where we are going ultimately, we can determine the direction in which we should like to move. We cannot discern the distant scene, but the immediate steps ahead are clear enough. And prayer in solitude, as well as common prayer, must evolve with reference to man's new understanding of himself as a phenomenon within biological space-time.

Prayer and Our Image of Man

We shall also have to bring our understanding and practice of prayer into some kind of harmony with the insights of depth psychology in our expanding world view. In the light of our newly acquired knowledge of the dynamics of repression and projection, we shall have to reconstruct our concept of the function of prayer in the attaining of personal wholeness and integrity. We know something about the compensating activities of the unconscious, offsetting and balancing deprivations of early childhood, and the "shadow" within who presents himself as an enemy to the conscious mind but who must be understood and embraced to be disarmed. We are grateful for the progress in self-understanding that has enabled us to see one of our favorite images of God as a projection of a quality of love some of us experienced in relation to our human fathers. But this does not explain away the source or the present function or final dénouement of that quality of love in the still evolving universe.

Prayer as the practice of consciously relating to the mysterious presence—at specific times with focus of attention, and at other times, in a more diffuse way, subliminally—may be the best means I have of getting myself together in psychological wholeness and health, and growing toward the realization of my best potential. I may, through prayer, evolve appropriately as an individual during my own brief span of life. We have recognized the problems attendant upon a literal understanding of God as a person who indwells me and my fellows as well as the rest of creation. We are necessarily speaking in metaphors, the language of religion no less than of poetry and other forms of art. We are trying to communicate about a profound mystery in human experience. We speak of a person and a presence because to do so seems more true to the experience than to use any other metaphor or word symbol. What I experience is more like a presence, a person, a Holy Spirit than any other imagined entity to which I can give a name.

I need not feel inwardly divided by this experience. The living religions provide me with something of a spiritual portrait, a psychological character sketch of this Person or Self, this God or Brahma, this Holy Spirit. And I experience at first hand his shadowy presence in the depths of my own being and that of others. My responsibility is to come to terms with him in myself, to get myself together in obedience to the demands he places upon me, and to become increasingly aware of his presence in others. As I undertake to do so, I find no conflict between this practice and the insights of modern depth psychology. Rather I am instructed and guided in my quest against pitfalls into which I should otherwise certainly stray. I find that by so doing I can be a fully modern man in Teilhard's sense and build for myself a world view that can at once accommodate the practice of inward prayer and the perspectives of evolution and depth psychology.

The "Lines of Maximum Coherence"

But if the practice of prayer is to remain "thinkable" and "true" for me in such a way that I can embrace it with renewed conviction and passion, I shall have to understand what I am doing within this new and inescapable context. My restored confidence will be born of a frank confession of the anguish into which I have first been plunged by these new perspectives and the religious impulse to bring the persistent experience of presence into some kind of harmony with them. No facile faith will suffice, no belief based on absurdity, no leap of faith in some kerygma I dare not demythologize, no acceptance of a Jesus I am not able to see as the final flower of a process which has been incarnational since its inception.

It is instructive to recollect that Teilhard arrived at his own great synthesis at the far side of a dark night that only the modern man whom he defined for us can know. First he had to confront a terror which in its magnitude and intensity paled even that experienced by Pascal. Let him rehearse for us the sequence that has an unmistakable autobiographical ring:

The child is terrified when it opens its eyes for the first time. Similarly, for our mind to adjust itself to lines and horizons enlarged beyond measure, it must renounce the comfort of familiar narrowness. It must create a new equilibrium for everything that had formerly been so neatly arranged in its small inner world. It is dazzled when it emerges from its dark prison, awed to find itself suddenly at

the top of a tower, and it suffers from giddiness and disori-
entation. The whole psychology of modern disquiet is
linked with the sudden confrontation with space-time. . . .
Conscious or not, suppressed anguish—a fundamental anguish of being—despite our smiles, strikes in the depths of
all our hearts and is the undertone of all our conversations.
. . . In the first and most widespread degree, the 'malady
of space-time' manifests itself as a rule by a feeling of futility, of being crushed by the enormities of the cosmos.[4]

Teilhard finds the "complement and necessary cor-
rective" to this malady: ". . . the perception of an evolution animating these dimensions. . . . Indeed time
and space become humanized as soon as a definite movement appears which gives them a physiognomy." [5]

For this "sickness of the dead end—the anguish of
feeling shut in," [6] and "of not being sure, and not seeing
how it (the modern world) ever could be sure that
there is an outcome—a suitable outcome—to that evolution" [7] there is a remedy: "We have only to think and
to walk in the direction in which the lines passed by
evolution take on their maximum coherence." [8]

Teilhard was committed to truth wherever it might
lead him. He would neither decline to weigh all the evidence nor tortuously bend evidence to conform to a preconceived faith. Nurtured in a Church that had
gathered together into one imagined adversary "the
world, the flesh, and the devil," he had the daring and
the independence to proclaim a new basis for faith:

If as a result of some interior revolution, I were success-
fully to lose my faith in Christ, my faith in a personal god,

my faith in the Spirit, I think that I would still continue to believe in the World. The World (the value, the infallibility, the goodness of the World): that, in the final analysis, is the first and the last thing in which I believe. It is by this faith that I live, and it is to this faith, I feel, that at the moment of death, mastering all doubts, I shall surrender myself. . . . I surrender myself to this undefined faith in a single and Infallible World, wherever it may lead me.[9]

In a world view culminating in a determination "to think and to walk in the direction in which the lines passed by evolution take on their maximum coherence" surely there is plausible place for prayer.

4

EXPANDING THE
DIMENSIONS OF PRAYER

WHILE IT MUST be reinterpreted for modern man, the practice of prayer can be justified within the framework of his current world view. The very perspectives of evolution and depth psychology which initially had tended to preclude the reasonableness and place of prayer in life actually provide, on deeper penetration into their implications, additional motivation for prayer, and demand new dimensions for the practice of prayer itself.

We have seen that there has been a radical displacement of man's vision of God with reference to space and time. There has also been the necessity to abandon certain metaphors relating to the nature of God that are no longer appropriate. Gone is the god "up there" or "out there." Gone forever is the god of a finished creation. Gone is the heavenly potentate whose vassal is man. Gone is the supreme judge sitting on his bench in the cosmic courtroom, meting out punishments and rewards and accepting a substitutionary propitiation from Christ for those sins of man for which no sentence could be sufficiently severe. Gone the heartless father who demands more of his children than they can possibly produce, who made man depraved and perverse, or at least capable of a calamitous "fall" into depravity and perversity, and then cruelly demands an impossible righteousness, eternal punishment being the penalty for inevitable failure. Gone the god who predestines for salvation his elect and consigns all others to hell. Gone the god who plays favorites even with his elect, capriciously answering some prayers while rejecting others. Fortunate the man for whom that composite god is indeed dead!

The God to Whom Modern Man Prays

The only God whom modern man can worship and address in prayer is the personalized source of, and energy for, a continuing creation, a within-ness "deep down things," which has already unfurled and opened up and evolved into human personality with its potential for goodness, compassion, and love. And the end of that opening out from within is not yet!

In what sense this immanent God is also transcendent is more difficult to define. At least one aspect of the transcendence is evidenced by the fact that in the evolutionary process the potential lies always beyond what has been actualized. Moreover, despite the element of unpredictability and contingency characteristic of the process, there must have been a kind of given-ness about the potential from the beginning. Of all universes, conceivable or inconceivable, this is the one we have. There is also the sense in which, in an evolving world, immanence and transcendence must be one. Transcendence, after all, can only be known as an inference through the experience of God's immanence in something or someone.

When I address as a person, in prayer, the source of the best that is in man and the as yet unrealized potential for goodness and greatness in man, I am admittedly making use of poetic license and thinking metaphorically. But if personality is the value most important to man, I may well stand in reverence and awe before the mystery that produced it and the promise of further development that remains within it. Within this phenomenon of personhood lies the intimation of the presence of a person who fulfills in himself what we see undeveloped and only by promise in man.

Prayer then is my response in praise, thanksgiving, confession, intercession, petition, adoration, and contemplation to an ideal person, companion, friend, whose being may be conjecture and projection, but who is also very real to me both in immanence and transcendence. In this way and up to this point we reconcile the experience of this presence and the perspective of evolution, thus making prayer the plausible exercise of relating our imperfect personhood to an imagined ideal person who embodies, in a developed and perfected manner, the best we have known in some persons.

We do well to obey the ancient counsel of Israel that we are not to make any graven image of God, not even to insist that he is a person. We can only say in our confusion and ignorance that this presence or mystery evokes from us responses that seem appropriate only when directed to some person-like being. How shall I express toward a thing the emotion I feel of awe and reverence and love? I am compelled to go on calling this mysterious presence a Being, God, or the Holy Spirit, knowing full well that he is to remain, finally, nameless and imageless.

The New Motivation for Prayer

Man is, therefore, blessed by his new understanding of the "immense journey" by which he has arrived at his present estate, and of the marvelous ecological interdependence and interpenetration of everything in a given environment and, indeed, in the total environment. Both the study of evolution—the process of ongoing creation in the dimension of time—and of ecology —the process in its dimension of simultaneity—suggest new contexts for, and new ways of, pursuing traditional forms of prayer.

Heretofore, prayer has been offered against a background that was taken to be relatively static. Theological notions of the purpose and function of prayer were cast as much in the Aristotelian mold of eternal essences

46

as in the Judaeo-Christian concepts of heaven and hell and of the ultimate Kingdom, brought to pass on earth by God's fiat (eschatology) without benefit of any evolutionary process. The motivation for prayer, apart from petitioning the Deity for daily bread and the well-being of one's enemies as well as those one loved, was to prepare a man to qualify for transport to heaven or for ultimate citizenship in the coming Kingdom on earth. Man was a man. His essence, for good or ill, had been determined. Within these limitations he could opt for heaven or hell as an eternal abode.

Now we know man has no eternal essence. He was not put here on this earth as he is. He's been a long time coming, and no one knows where he's going from here. What is the essence of something that is evolving? Its first state, or its last, or somewhere in between? Who shall determine? Moreover, the fully "modern" man can no longer entertain any notion of a divine intervention, truncating history and establishing a new social order on earth. Neither do traditional images of heaven and hell as specific places in space seem viable to him within his current world view. He may hold out hope for, even expectation of, some survival of the individual beyond death, so long as he is not asked to image this in any particular way. But his motivation for prayer must no longer *derive* from these sources.

Prayer as the most effective means to a larger, richer life here and now, a way of becoming more fully alive in this present, may still appeal to him. And, in proportion to his empathic capacity to identify with the entire evolutionary process and its current ecological dimension, he is given a powerful new motivation for prayer. From evolution he has learned that the origin of new species has its roots in the creative adaptation of the individuals within the species. From the beginning there has been concealed within evolving life the potential which, in unbroken interaction with the ecological complex through these eons of time, has had this present realization in man's branch of the tree of life.

The conviction inevitably grows on him that there must still lie within man a hidden potential to become the new man, man's successor, the son of man. He realizes further that movement in this direction for the species has to take place first by mutation within the individual. In prayer a man can meditate upon the nature of the being he would become, reaching toward it in spirit and aspiration. In some sense he may adore the imageless Holy Spirit whom this next step would a little more adequately incarnate.

The New Role of Adoration

Thus adoration itself becomes the leverage for movement forward. The ever elusive, imageless image of the Holy Spirit is the star to which, in prayer, man attaches his little wagon. But he is not under the strain of *pulling* alone. The entire momentum of the evolutionary process and its hidden potential are also *pushing* from behind and from within. We speak of the gravitational pull of the moon. But the tide also develops its own momentum and it is in the nature of water to be free to flow. In prayer man has a chance to become a forerunner. He has a chance to become another brother of the first-born. He can experience, at least by promise, the thrill of the new life. This is the life-giving reward of this kind of prayer for the individual here and now.

At the same time, he is aware that what he is doing is engaging in an act of intercession on behalf of all mankind. His "work" of prayer is a labor of love that *counts* for the species in the bringing to birth of the new species, the new man. Prayer then is not only for the sake of achieving, by the grace of God, his own immediate salvation (release from all that would enslave or bog him down, prevent his entrance into a new life-style, foreshadowing that of the new man) but also for the sake of his fellow man. He consecrates himself—on behalf of all men who now live and who are yet to be born.

Heretofore, mutations have come about through unconscious experimentation and effort in directions opened by convergence of inner potential and outer opportunity. Some reptiles had it in them to become birds. Individuals achieved gradual proximations. The accumulated effort of individuals within a species produced the new species. Eventually reptiles literally sprouted wings and became birds. The three-toed horse had it in him to adapt to a life on the plains, where speed was useful, by moving so much and for so long on his middle toe as to develop in time into the fleet-footed horse of today, galloping on the single toe that has become a hoof.

Loren Eiseley speaks of the tree shrew that once contained, by potential, the possibility of man.[1] Once that prehistoric animal "contained" man, but man is long since "gone." What does man now contain by promise that wants "out," "to be gone"? Here is matter for meditation, together with the exercise of deliberate choice among possibilities and a consequent movement of the will. Movement in a new direction was, until man's arrival, unconscious. Henceforth, in man the movement may be deliberately chosen and self-consciously taken. And the power to move, I am suggesting, may well be the prayer of adoration.

Cultivating Ecological Awareness

We have been speaking primarily here of the process in its dimension of time. We must not lose sight of the process in the dimension of simultaneity which is the ecological interpenetration and interdependence of everything in the environment. The mystics in actual experience have anticipated the insights and knowledge of the ecologists. They *knew* they were one with all about them in their strange experience of undifferentiated unity, without having any scientific knowledge of the extent of actual interpenetration. "Dust thou art and dust thou shalt become." "Ashes to ashes and dust to dust." But what tremendous extension of these concepts our current vision of life, springing out of matter and returning to matter, has afforded!

We are bound into a biosphere encircling the globe itself, a super-organism in which all separate living things co-inhere. All this cellular substance has sprung from the molecular substance in the matter of the earth, and continues to draw sustenance from it and to evolve by the "grace" of its presence. In addition, men have created a superimposed "noosphere"—a thought membrane comprised of ideas, cultural patterns, ideologies, religions. Continuing evolution is even now taking place within the inconceivable complexity of the ecological situation in every passing moment.

Hence man's growing concern for the maintenance of an ecological balance, both in the biosphere and the noosphere, that will be favorable to his present survival and his future evolution. First he needs to know with his mind and to experience existentially how everything in the environment affects everything else for good or ill, in terms of his survival and the continuance of his evolution as a species. Once this reality dawns on him with the force of "revelation," he is a changed man. He becomes an instant conservationist, with a passion! He is driven to fight pollution as the mortal enemy it is. He is concerned for population control, whether by self-discipline or the means of contraception. He necessarily becomes an internationalist, putting far above any national interest the family of man. The preservation of the species becomes his present preoccupation, its further development his ultimate concern.

The central fascination of life becomes the great concept of the continued "hominisation" of man, man becoming the man he has it in him to be, given the maintenance of a favorable environment, physical, social, and ideological. His new prayer becomes the recollection of his condition in time and space, the mystical identification with the rest of creation, and deep personal involvement of the affections and will in adoration of man's ever-coming, ever-expanding, ever-receding vision of the Holy Spirit.

No one has shown us how to meditate upon the past and present dimensions of continuing evolution (which is continuing creation) as sensitively and effectively as Loren Eiseley. He expresses no religious faith, embraces no ritualistic practice, yet his writing breathes the most profound religious experience. I suppose one might call it the religion of contemporary mystical humanism or humanistic mysticism. To read his books, which constitute a new form of devotional literature, is to be quickened in motivation for this quest and to be taught how to pursue it. His essays reflect the shape this kind of prayer we are commending has taken for one man, blessed with a wonderful combination of scientific knowledge and mystical capacity. He would be very reluctant to admit that he is engaging in prayer. He is very reticent in speaking of his God. He would not presume to choose a direction and to persuade others to pursue it with him. But the reality of all these commitments is there by implication. There is no didactic preaching; at the same time, the quiet persuasion is irresistible.

This new context for prayer which is emerging quite naturally in human experience to meet our new understanding of ourselves requires for our sustained awareness of it more or less rhythmic times of solitude, close to nature, undisturbed by the distractions of urban life. Modern urban civilization conceals from us both our roots and the processes of interaction and interpenetration by which we live and breathe. We need to recover the sense of where we really are in time and space, a feeling for biological space-time, the actual duration in which we are participant. Within this newly grasped context we must train ourselves to catch fleeting glimpses of the man we are to be in order that mankind may give birth to the son of man.

Already we dimly perceive some of the necessary ingredients: nonviolence (*Satyagraha* or soul-force); more profound self-knowledge in the light of depth-psychological insights; commitment to the family of man as distinct from any race, nation, or present political ideology; the cultivation of mystical identification with all men in order that compassion may be quickened, as well as the will to apply it in action to the end of social reform. The motivation and the destination are the same: the elusive, not-to-be-imaged, Holy Spirit of God. And the energy is adoration. God, buried in the depths of our own humanity, we must learn to adore.

Depth Psychology and Prayer

Of course, if God is himself only the projection of a father image, then the whole business of prayer is doomed to futility from the outset. And if prayer is but the unconscious continuation into later life of childhood patterns of dependency, clearly I had better stop it and begin to grow up. To help negotiate this transition for those who can afford it, the prone posture on the psychiatrist's couch replaces the kneeling posture in the oratory, and the dependency on the father image is transferred for the time being from God to the psychiatrist.

One's image of almighty God may indeed have been too much influenced by associations with one's human father, stored in the unconscious. But this need not of itself justify the death of my God by an act of deliberate deicide. When I amend my notions of the nature of God on the basis of deeper self-knowledge of what took place in my childhood and its influence upon my ideas of him, I may still find the great conjecture, now refined, justified by human experience. There is nothing, after all, in psychology capable of disproving the existence of God as an imageless Holy Spirit whose operation is uniquely revealed to and through the mind of man.

My own conviction is that we have a very great deal of benefit to derive from thorough acquaintance with the insights arising from modern depth psychology. I recognize that they are of an order equivalent, in terms of revelation, to the concepts of the evolutionary process of which they are one aspect. Indeed they deal with the whole evolution of man's psyche and its present stage of development in response to the current ecological context of social as well as material environment. Psychiatry has always had as its objective the integration of the individual human personality. The study of evolution has identified the criterion of advance as the phenomenon of ever more remarkable unification in the presence of ever greater complexity in the development of the organism. The function of depth-psychological inquiry is in accordance with the *élan vital* of the whole evolutionary process.

We have been insisting, at the same time, that religion, as the impulse to bind everything into one bundle, is the focal point of this crucial force in man. A man's religion is the way he "puts it all together," whether his religion be primitive, false, or highly developed and true in the correspondence of its metaphors to the reality of expanding experience. Further, if the life blood of religion is prayer, then prayer and depth-psychological insights must get together in some effective way. They are working toward the same end: greater individuation and integration.

Man needs to know in psychological terms what is happening generally in the successive stages of his life's development. He needs to know about the early oral and genital orientations, their associations with the persons who made the earliest and therefore, in some respects, the deepest impression on his life. He needs to understand the carry-over in the unconscious of both the satisfactions and deprivations of the period of infancy and early childhood. He needs to be familiar with the evidence of, and the patterns taken by, the necessary identity quest in late childhood and adolescence, of the way in which true maturity must be understood, psychologically, as the achievement of integrity.

It would be a great thing if every person in early adulthood had access to a good analyst for at least a year to help him identify and work through the forces operative in his own infancy and childhood. It would be still better, less confusing and traumatic, if the analyst had, like Carl Jung, a genuine respect for religion and its most distinctive phenomenon, prayer. And if he operated, as some do, within the consciousness of a triangular relationship between himself, his patient, and God. Of course such a happy opportunity is available to very few people. Those who can afford it should be careful to select an analyst who shares, as far as possible, the same values and can therefore appreciate the patient's aspirations, and who has a genuine respect for and acceptance of the validity of religious experience, even if he or she does not think of himself as a religious person. Teilhard, in a letter to Père August Valensin, recalled the testimony of St. Teresa: "There are plenty of confessors, but where can you find anyone who really knows you? You meet him only once or twice in your life."

If most of us are denied the benefit of a trained analyst as confessor, we can at least seek until we find a person who is conversant with the psychological phenomena we have refererd to. We can read, reflect upon, and apply to ourselves the kind of material presented in the growing literature produced within the interdisciplinary field of psychology and religion. We can respond to opportunities to become part of groups where there can be mutual stimulation in what must remain, in its deeper and wider dimension, essentially a solitary quest.

The insights we have reference to require what amounts to a revolutionary change in our understanding of what is to happen in the practice of prayer. New techniques are being offered by psychologists for the pursuit of individuation and integration which, taken together, can be said to provide new forms of traditional prayer. Consider the kind of *experiment in depth* P. W. Martin is proposing in his book by this title, gathering, interrelating, and applying the insights of T. S. Eliot, Carl Jung, and Arnold Toynbee to the discipline we are describing. This can be seen of course as a fully secular, psychological pursuit. But this is not the case when the objective is personal salvation from one's hang-ups and release to live a larger life in whatever terms these are described, *and* when one also chooses to embark on the experiment in depth "under the aspect of the eternal" and for the sake of God and one's fellow man as well as oneself. Is the pursuit not then a legitimate form of prayer? If I experience myself as inseparably united with *the Self* in some indefinable way, does not my quest of integrated selfhood involve deep-going communion with my God at every point?

If the experiment in depth may be considered, by the man who orients himself in religious terms, a prayer of individuation and integration, mark how easily an identification may be made between the *daimon* in the unconscious, who stands ready to lead us into truth about ourselves, and the immanent God who dwells within. Without denying the truth of Freud's contention that the unconscious reveals the pathology of neurotic illness, Jung insisted that it also contained the positive secret as to the way ahead into greater individuation as well as the power to achieve new integration—in other words, the home of a daimon that can be trusted. While the unconscious is the repository of repressions—the arena where conflicts are taking place of which the conscious mind is unaware—it is also the ground of our being and contains the pearl of great price: the seed of our unification and development. When we want to know what is responsible for our torn-to-pieces-ness, we must consult the unconscious. When we want to know how to get ourselves together in a creative way that is also viable for us as individual persons, again we must consult the unconscious!

From the point of view of the mystical approach to religious experience this counsel makes a great deal of sense. George Fox did not believe any more passionately in the capacity of the Inner Light (the Seed, he sometimes called it) to reveal to a man the truth about himself than did Carl Jung with regard to the unconscious. I believe they were talking about the same experience from different perspectives and in different terms.

One who today attempts to see the world in religious terms must, as a post-Darwinian man, make a radical adjustment in his time perspective. The God of a once finished creation must now be seen as God still at work. Knowledge of the process of evolution has revealed that the growing edge of this process is where new and wider forms of awareness and consciousness are evolving; it is at the point where God must still be shaping man from within the unconscious. If this is so for the species, it must also hold for the individual man. As a post-Freudian man, he must also look upon the unconscious as the point at which God provides him the best glimpse of the present state of his own soul—but also, and this is of great importance, as the place where God chooses to reveal the clues about what must be set right and about the directions in which further growth is to come.

These clues have to do with relationships that must be changed and redeemed. They also may point to a neglected potential. If prayer at its best is overhearing the converse between the Father and the Son, this is perhaps the deepest level at which we can become attentive to it. The voice of the daimon in the unconscious and the voice of God are one voice. It is not merely something; it is someone who is trying to say something to me through my unconscious. I shall, by the grace of God, learn to be attentive. As one individual in the evolving phenomenon of man I shall rejoice to experiment with the evolving phenomenon of prayer.

5

BECOMING

ATTENTIVE TO THE SPIRIT

THE UNDERSTANDING of the nature of prayer, which I have been putting forward, has been in terms of a conscious relationship to a person-like being, God or Holy Spirit, whose presence is made known in human experience. The God of each man's prayers will be different because he is differently known to each: he is the God of Abraham, the God of Isaac, and the God of Jacob. I know him through what others have told me of him in their experience. But he is also my God, whom I have come to know in the uniqueness of my own interior experience.

Taking Time to Know God

My first responsibility, then, if I am to be serious about praying, is to devote time regularly to coming to know my God. There undoubtedly are some once-born men, as William James described them, who may be able to sustain a consciousness of the presence without any need to discipline themselves by taking some time every day, apart and alone, with concentration of attention, for the specific purpose of praying. But those of us who know we must be reborn over and over again, need to set aside a time to pray every day, preferably at the same hour, and, insofar as possible, in the same place. I should hope to grow increasingly into a more sustained awareness of the presence, but I shall be able to do so only if I quite deliberately take some time, every day if possible, to be alone with my God.

Many of us find this very first requirement a great stumbling block. We are harassed by an ever expanding, self-imposed set of responsibilities and standards of self-improvement. In no other area does the popular conscience make such cowards of us all. The conformist, competitive aspects of our nature resent an allotment of time and energy which bears so little direct evidence of productivity. We are far more driven than most of us ever realize by the fear, mostly unconscious, that if we step aside from the active pursuit of our work, others will get ahead and we shall never catch up. There is also the illusion that there will be more time in some mythical future, and that if we will just keep busy now we shall have somehow earned a respite later on. We shall then be able to devote time in an unhurried way to some of the practices we intend to cultivate. Alas, the expected time never comes. This hope turns out to be illusory because a sense of the presence of God becomes more and more difficult to recover, and the knowledge of his words and ways begins to fade into an unreal and seemingly unrelated past. If we would know this elusive companion, we must first spend a good deal of time with him, consistently and ungrudgingly.

Every successive stage of mental prayer, from the first movement to the last, as well as that inward and sustained posture that might be described as praying without ceasing, involves what has been classically called meditation. But meditation is a very inclusive word. All reflection is meditation of a kind. It can be quite profane. Do we not speak even of premeditated *murder?* Meditation becomes prayer when what I am reflecting upon I consciously relate to my God. If I try to see the matter from his point of view, to find him in it, or to find his will regarding it, my meditation becomes prayer. This is why I call this central and crucial prayer of meditation the practice of "thinking God's thoughts after him." No form of mental or verbal prayer, in which the intellect is active in any way, escapes that demand.

Meditation is a quest for God himself and a knowledge of his Word. "In the beginning was the Word, and the Word was with God, and the Word was God." To attempt to think God's thoughts after him is a passion to know the Word. Man is distinguished from all other creatures by his ability to understand, at least in a measure, and to respond to the Word. We could not come to know one another in any depth without words. We can retain the memory and the image of a man after his death, apart from visual reproductions, only through words he has spoken and written, and through words others have spoken and written about him. Words from which ideas are shaped are the food of meditation, spoken or unspoken. To meditate is to think, to reflect, to relate words and ideas to each other. It is the work of the mind under the direction of the heart. To engage in this work in order to know God and his will for us, to put our precious treasury of words to the express purpose of discovering and responding in obedience to the Word, this is the prayer of meditation. How shall I otherwise come to know him who *is* the Word?

The Analogy of Human Friendship

We shall find throughout this attempt to understand prayer and to reawaken a desire to pursue it that the basic and recurring analogy is, inevitably, human friendship. The deepest friendship is the experience of being in love. The experience, as all who have been in love know, involves the inward process of referring all one sees and reflects upon to the consciousness of the other's presence, even when the beloved is not there. It is an effortless process, requiring neither will nor discipline. It is as natural as breathing and as inescapable. The lover sees what he sees with the eyes of the beloved as well as his own. He hears what others say with her ears, and something in him responds in her accustomed way. He responds at once for himself and for her, and the interplay is a communion with her presence in the mind and heart. He thinks her thoughts after her, on her behalf, for his own sake as well as hers. As long as he remains in love, it is pure delight. When the process fades, he knows he is no longer "in love," no matter how much of respect and honor and admiration remains. In a similar way, prayer without ceasing is an unending love affair with the Holy Spirit.

But before that enchanted life can become a reality the twice and many-times born must come to know the Holy Spirit by a disciplined meditation on the Word and its demands. To the lover the beloved is a person. The lover knows her characteristic gestures and movements. He studies with anticipation her countenance. He recognizes the love light in her eyes and he knows, with wonder and awe and the deepest humility, that he alone is able to draw it forth in just this way. He knows the smile, the frown, the whole gamut of expression, reflecting pain, sorrow, query, recognition, love, joy. Above all he knows, cherishes, and rehearses to himself the *words*, the words she has spoken only to him. He knows also the words that are somehow characteristic of her, words others may use, perhaps, but never as she uses them, with the special inflection and nuance that is hers alone. The Holy Spirit, on the other hand, has no body of his own, no countenance; he can speak no words with a remembered tone and inflection. Intense concentration and earnest quest is therefore required before one can begin to know this shadowy companion and to respond to his presence.

It might be said that what the lover retains of the beloved in her absence is the inward image of her spirit. He sees with the mind's eye the face, the smile, the expression of the eyes, and the characteristic movement of the body. But what becomes central in consciousness when she is not actually present is something more diffuse, nonrepresentational, essentially imageless: her spirit. The experience is instructive. We are not to image God, and we may think of him as a person only with the knowledge that he is not really a person as a man is a person, and that we do so only because we are driven to use this metaphor for one who has no countenance and must remain forever the ultimate mystery.

But nevertheless, he can be konwn in the only way that is necessary for our soul's health. He can be known and recollected in solitude in the same way the lover keeps company with the beloved in her absence: by being conscious of her spirit. God has made himself known to us in the only way man has ever recognized him: through the presence of his Holy Spirit. Diffuse, nonrepresentational, abstract yet paradoxically recognizable, knowable, and, to him who has come to love God, more real, finally, than all else besides. Faceless, without eyes, and having no lips with which to pronounce words, he can speak to us from many faces, peer at us through many eyes, and speak every tongue with infinitely varied accent and inflection. And when we are alone his Holy Spirit is there, seeking us, awaiting our discovery and response.

Meditation on Scripture

This Holy Spirit speaks to us through passages in the scriptures of all the living religions. We do well to ponder the words sacred to other religions if only to recognize that the spiritual profile of this being, variously represented, is always the same, and to wonder at the marvel that he has not left himself without witness at any time nor in any place. But we also do well to become especially familiar with our own Bible, which contains for us the words that historically have conveyed his Word in the West. Words which reflect the Holy Spirit are distinguishable from other words in the Bible. We come increasingly to discern when he is the speaker, no matter who serves as his mouthpiece in the particular setting or drama.

His Word is the moral law that some of the characters in this drama respond to as the most important factor in their own development. So the psalmist confesses, "I meditate on thy law day and night," knowing full well that his real life, that is, his eternal life, depends upon obedience to this law. It is a matter of life and death. The specific laws in the book of Leviticus may or may not reflect this law. The man who meditates upon it day and night will have no great difficulty recognizing the difference. Jesus may have been the first to say specifically, "It hath been said by them of old times, but I say unto you . . ." But Jeremiah and other prophets before him had the same inner assurance that they could distinguish between the minutiae of the law and the law inscribed upon the hearts of men by the Holy Spirit.

Those who were practiced in this art of meditation upon *the* Law—the Word, that is—day and night, were perfectly clear that obedience to this law was more important to a man's well-being than either his estate or his health.

This law is not an abstract codicil but the inflexible *will* of God operating within his creation, inseparable from his Holy Spirit. Reflecting upon this *will* was one way, an essential way, the great figures of the Bible communed with the Holy Spirit. Pretending that one could live in opposition to it or unmindful of its operation was the ultimate folly. In the Old Testament the elders of Israel had the wisdom to see that sin was not so much the result of evil as the fruit of folly. We would think it foolish for a man to leap from a high building and not expect to perish. But the keenness of our sense of what constitutes spiritual folly has been blunted. It would be easier to be good if we could perceive as readily as the prophets how utterly foolish it is to violate the law that is the Word of the Holy Spirit. David knew when he ran afoul of the Word. Do we and our political leaders have the same moral judgment?

What we need to observe particularly here is that this meditation upon the Law of God, the Word of his Holy Spirit, was not a cringing obeisance. Certainly there was an element of fear and trembling in it, considering the penalties of banishment from the presence. But this practice of meditation was far more a delight than a dread. It was what men in their right minds *chose* to do because they wanted to. It was the first and most essential way of knowing God, so that one might come to love him. The fear of the Lord was the beginning of wisdom, then as now. It entailed respect for his law, conveyed in the Word. The wise man who has turned his back upon folly is able to say, "Thy will is my peace." As the lover rejoices to please the beloved, so the man of God seeks to know and to obey the will of him he has learned to love more dearly than life itself. Keeping company with this companion of the interior life is first and last a matter of seeking to know and wanting to respond to his will. Before this law there is no other.

Meditating on this law day and night is not a matter of reciting the commandments. It is a matter of seeing what the will that represents the mind of the Holy Spirit requires of one in specific relationships and under special circumstances, here, where one stands, now, at this moment. To think God's thoughts after him is not to wander afield in vain imaginings. It is to see one's present position under the aspect of the eternal, to lead the utterly open life before the beloved, to experience the divine simultaneity in which one harmonizes and integrates, in this lived moment, all of one's relationships and responsibilities. This applies not merely to one's own life, as if it could be lived in isolation from one's fellows; God's will is always seen within the context of God's will for Israel, his people, the whole community.

He who would be a man of prayer must regularly return to the Bible as a point of embarkation for his meditation because, for one who stands in our tradition, the Bible is the place where the primary lode is to be mined. Here, more than in any other book, the continuity of a peculiar people's discovery of the nature and demand of the Word, across a thousand years of un-flagging inquiry, is recorded with faithfulness and understanding. We see men struggling to know the Word in the intensity of their individual experience and on behalf of the beloved community. We see them succeeding in varying degree. We identify with the persons in the drama, speak their lines with them, lose ourselves in their struggle only to find ourselves again in the unfolding plot and to learn the will of the same Holy Spirit for our immediate need. We see the inescapable parallels and are forced to acknowledge the plumb line which measures the deviation of our society as truly as it stood in judgment upon the institutions of Israel. When we keep faithful company with the figures of the Bible in their quest for knowledge of God's holy will we learn to know ourselves and to see the issues of our time from the perspective of the Holy Spirit. This is one way we come to know their companion, who is also our companion, and to love him with our whole soul, mind, heart, and strength. Loving him, we shall learn, little by little, to think his thoughts after him, the thoughts that speak the Word to our individual lives and to our time and place.

One reads the Bible and reflects upon it not only to become familiar with the operation of the moral law but also to reflect upon the great range of potential for creativity within it and to glorify its author and to enjoy him forever. The fear of the Lord is only the *beginning* of wisdom. Its purpose is in part to teach us to recognize folly and to avoid it. But the *pursuit* of wisdom is a far more rewarding vocation than the negative avoidance of wrongdoing. To grow in wisdom is to grow in stature even if this does not always entail growing in favor with one's fellow man.

Wisdom, in view of the ever-expanding horizons for the creative play of imagination, as well as the opportunity for action which it opens up, is its own reward. It makes possible a life more abundant in its satisfactions and enrichments. As we identify and role-play in meditation with the men and women of the Bible, who grow before our eyes in their capacity to move skillfully and effortlessly in harmony with the moral law, we sense the invigoration and joy of a new freedom. We experience with Paul of Tarsus what he meant by the vivid image of scales falling from his eyes as he moved from the bondage of the old laws to the large freedom of the law of love.

Meditating on the Kingdom

What Jesus of Nazareth can do for those who would be his disciples now is just what he could do for his followers then: teach them how to live now in the Kingdom. The Kingdom of God has not come on earth in any of the existing social institutions of man. But this Kingdom did come in the life the Nazarene led, and it can come in a deep and releasing fashion for those who are drawn positively to the quality of life it offers and are prepared to follow the demands it makes. The Kingdom of God, Jesus told us, is within us. That is to say, in the perspective of our time, the capacity to understand, to respond, and to enter into the life-style of the

Kingdom is part of the built-in, given equipment of the species, man. The Kingdom is also in our midst, among us. That is to say, for centuries, perhaps for millennia, the Kingdom has been experienced by man momentarily as an actual *happening* in a recognizable quality of human relationship between man and man.

What marked Jesus apart from other men was the degree to which he was able to live in this Kingdom himself and his ability to interpret it for other men. If he had anything in him that might strike others as arrogance, it was the supreme confidence that he knew precisely what the Kingdom of God was like and what a man had to do to claim his citizenship in it. There are athletes who achieve in a particular sport such a degree of perfection that their movements create an illusion of effortlessness. They make the difficult look easy. They develop an inward confidence, occasionally even before it has been justified by performance. When a certain prize fighter announced publicly that he was "the greatest," some found the implied arrogance unbearable until achievement made them concede that the claim was not excessive. But it was the athlete himself who knew, even before he proved it to others, that he had the capacity. I remember reading the Gospel of Mark quietly at one sitting, when leisure following an operation afforded the opportunity, and being struck by a comparable arrogance in this athlete of the spirit, Jesus of Nazareth. The tone and manner of his pronouncements seemed to be saying very clearly by implication, "When it comes to knowing what the Kingdom of God is all about and to being able to interpret it for others,

I'm the greatest." Only gradually and reluctantly do we come to concede the point.

We read and ponder the events and the teaching in the life of Jesus to learn something about the life-style which is, indeed, the Kingdom within and amongst men. There are very strict rules to this game, and one can very easily disqualify himself by violating them. These are made apparent in the accounts. But what makes some want to accept and to obey them is the irresistible appeal of the life-style the Kingdom represents. It is comparable to an earlier age, paleontologically, when a few venturesome reptiles were motivated, in spite of the dead weight of immemorial conformity, to abandon the earth and to take flight as birds. Some men, still evolving, are so drawn to "take wings" and enter the "new environment" that they are able to exert their energies and strive inwardly to move toward functioning in the new element, the Kingdom.

The difference between flaccid acquiescence in a lower level of life and bestirring oneself to gain admission into the new realm is, in part, a sustained practice of meditation upon the nature of the Kingdom. It is a readiness to sit patiently at the feet of one who never tired of composing new parables to follow hard upon the often repeated words "the Kingdom of heaven is like . . ." It was a very different business from the somber proclamations of a John the Baptist. It was the passionate compulsion, the magnificent obsession of one who knew that cultivating the capacity to live in the Kingdom had made all the difference to him, and whose bread and wine was the joy of bringing others into the same promised land. Meditation whose objective is entrance into the Kingdom *now,* in spirit and in truth, would do well to return regularly to the waters of this spring for refreshment and renewal of the sense of direction.

Other Nutriment for Meditation

While the Bible in the foreseeable future will hold this central place in the practice of meditation for those who stand in the Christian tradition, there is an ever-accumulating treasure of devotional literature that can now nourish more than one lifetime of every seeker after the Kingdom. Every man must find those writers who speak peculiarly to his condition. He shall not discover who they are unless he explores the field for himself. There are, of course, the great classics which have spoken to countless men for centuries, including St. Augustine's *Confessions; The Imitation of Christ; The Theological Germanica; The Little Flowers of St. Francis;* the writings of St. John of the Cross, of St. Teresa of Avila, and of Jacob Boehme, as well as those of the English mystics, William Law, William Blake, Julian of Norwich, and others. Some find greater contemporaneity in the more recent writings of Soren Kierkegaard, Baron Von Hügel, Dean Inge, Evelyn Underhill, Thomas Kelly, or Rufus Jones. One finds, by experimentation, his own special friends of the spirit. It is a good thing to stay with one's own guru once discovered, at least as long as his teaching can still be received with some experience of freshness and wonder. And, of course, we must expand our horizons to include material for meditation from the new literature that reflects the evolutionary and ecological dimensions.

Many have noted that once one enters upon the pilgrimage under competent guides, the coincidence of happening upon just the right book, affording the right counsel and insight at the right time, seems extraordinarily providential. It is as if the Holy Spirit were secretly at work in us, planning for us our future, never-ending education in the *way*. Each new teacher points us to others who have influenced him. Under the tutelage and mysterious prompting of those who are "given" us to show us where to look for him, how to recognize him, and how to express the love we feel for him, we come increasingly to think God's thoughts after him. The last movement of every valid meditation makes us aware of the growing edge within, involving changes in relationships, attitudes, and vocational direction.

Again, the haunting question returns: What if my God, this dear companion, at once within and beyond, were but the voice of the being man has it in him to become, drawing him irresistibly forward? In response I yet would need to query why, of all possible worlds, there is such an one as this, whence springs man? And whither does he tend? This man-to-be, man's successor, the son of man, would still be my Lord, if not my God, in some profound sense. On the other hand, if there is such a God as Western man has conceived, then he is, of course, infinitely beyond and *other than* any person who has ever lived. His ways are not our ways; they are past finding out. Yet both the hint of his existence and such qualities as we conjecture are his are suggested to us only by what we know of man's potential or at least what springs from his imagination. In either case, we return as ever to the conclusion that this being, neither ourselves nor any other man, yet within us all and far beyond any of us, elicits from us a spirit of wonder, awe and adoration. In my unique experience of him he becomes *my* God, and I am constrained, if I would become and remain myself, to think his thoughts after him.

6

CELEBRATING THE

CONTINUING CREATION

WHEN THE MIND and spirit have been prepared for prayer through unhurried reflection upon some passage of Scripture or devotional writing that gently leads one into the presence of his God, making transition from focus on the secular to focus on the sacred, the next movement of prayer may well be one of celebration. I call it celebration, rather than praise, to suggest the elements of spontaneity and originality that ought to characterize our present rehearsal of the traditional form. "The Lord is in his holy temple. Let all the earth keep silence before him." "The Lord is in me, for my body is the temple of his Holy Spirit. Let all my being keep silence before him." "This is the day which the Lord hath made. I will rejoice and be glad in it."

If we have nothing to celebrate, we are of all men the most miserable. And unless we learn to recollect the mood of celebration, we shall have to await its fitful and only occasional return. Is this a form of self-hypnosis? Certainly it is a willed determination to recover, in God's presence, a sense of joy in his continuing creation. The persistent stream of consciousness is at the mercy of every passing stimulus, interior and exterior. In this exercise in celebration we allow this stream of consciousness the breathing space to be influenced by the recollection of the numinous, the holy, the mysterious source of all that we should like to celebrate in this life.

Behold, It Is Very Good!

We recover God's own mood as reflected in the imagination of one of the authors of the Book of Genesis: "God saw everything that He had made, and behold it was very good." That's celebration! Speaking in metaphors about a supposed beginning no one as yet knows anything about, this unknown author projects himself into the existential experience of one who may have been the author of all that is. By a superb leap of insight, confirmed by our imaginative capacity to role-play the Creator, he thinks God's thoughts after him, speaks what he imagines to have been his words, after him: "Behold, it is very good!" From our point of view it isn't only that what had been created was indeed very good, it is that this exclamation, this interior excitement and joy, was an important and inherent part of this very good beginning. Again, it is only in metaphors that we speak. There may have been no alpha point and there may be no omega point, no beginning nor any end, despite the demands imposed by our finite minds.

Bad as our contemporary world with its problems may be, bad as the personal predicament of any individual man may be, we know that we should not be telling it entirely "like it is" if we did not make room at the beginning of our prayer for this note of celebration. I know there are some persons who, humanly speaking, would seem to have nothing to celebrate. Misfortune has dealt them irreparable blows. Physical or mental handicaps may preclude the mood of celebration. It would be blasphemy to chide them for inability to respond to this call. But unless one's childhood was exceedingly deprived both of love and of pleasure, one has retained, at least in recollection, the feeling of what it was like to be glad to be alive.

> Bliss was it then to be alive.
> And to be young was very heaven.[1]

Well then, in this first movement of our faltering and always unfinished symphony of prayer, let us recollect that mood. Let us say the words of praise that others have bequeathed to us from happy tongues that knew how to shape them well. Let us also assay our own phrases, stumbling and stammering as they may be. Once on a time we created some little thing with our hands or our speech which pleased us. We remember that we too, however presumptuous the comparison may seem, exclaimed inwardly or outwardly, "Behold, it is very good!" or its equivalent. We celebrated in that moment. In that moment, however, unlike him at other times, we were certainly recognizable as made in the image of this God whose intuitive response, we are told, at the first great occasion of invention, was also to celebrate.

Perhaps what we most want to offer praise for is precisely the possibility of invention, of surprise, of something new under the sun. Of all possible universes the imagination might conceive, we have this one and no other. That calls for celebration! That we have a universe at all—that calls for another round of celebration! That it is a uni-verse, totally integrated instead of chaotic—yet another! That we are here as participants, amid the staggering odds against man's arrival, much less our own—further celebration. This celebration may not inappropriately have some element in it of Peter Pan's exultant spirit as he sings, in the musical version of the play, "I can crow." Not that, of ourselves, we have anything to crow about in a universe we did not create. But as one of God's creatures, made in some inescapable sense in the divine image, perhaps we are entitled to some vicarious crowing. In any case, I am suggesting that it is this irresistible, irrepressible spirit of exuberant celebration that affords an auspicious beginning for the traditional sequence of the movements of prayer.

Moreover, we post-Darwinian men of the twentieth century have been given an unearned increment to our celebration. Former generations of men thought original creation was completed. God at the very beginning had made everything that is—and that was that! Celebration was in order for the Creator, of course. But men had to project themselves backward infinitely in time in order to participate vicariously. Now all this is changed. Creation is unfinished. It continues to take place before our very eyes. Life is still evolving on this planet.

The finger of God in Michelangelo's extraordinary painting of the Creation has not yet been withdrawn from the finger tip of Adam. Unwitting genius that lends itself to the interpretations of a new age! Instead of an extrinsic creation, we now can envisage an intrinsic one. The visual image must change. God reaches up through the still unfolding consciousness of man from the inside, still shaping the unfinished man, the man that is to be, the new man. We were not present at the first creation. We *are* present at the creation still taking place in the ever-present now. We are entitled to think God's thoughts after him and to shout with him, "Behold, it is very good!" Hallelujah!

Called to Be Co-Creators

Nor do we participate as guilty bystanders and spectators alone. There is much that is already given that we can celebrate on God's behalf as well as our own. But our celebration has been afforded a new dimension. We are co-creators. We may see that at least in certain crucial successions of events "all things have worked together for good until now" in the divine providence. But now we have an important share in the responsibility to see that they should continue to work together for good in man's further development.

However unbelievable and awesome the thought may be, reflection confirms that creation is still taking place in and through individual men. We too, under God, are miniature creators. We are commissioned to participate in the unfinished creation of ourselves. We are given a daily opportunity to behold and to be able to say with appropriate reservations and tentativeness, "Behold, it is very good!" It would be, however, a trivial and insignificant creation if only ourselves were involved. What is at stake in this continuing creation is the species man and his community on earth. In our tiny sphere of influence within our families and circles of friends, vocational and avocational interests, we may help to build the species for good or ill.

Nor is this an insignificant opportunity. Species have come about only through the efforts of individuals. The individual in any species which adapted in a new creative way to its environment—what science has called a "sport"—has been the fulcrum which moved at that point the whole direction of evolution. Evolution has at last become conscious of itself in man. He is the first animal capable of determining what direction he may choose for his unfinished evolution.

Someone has said "man is condemned to meaning." From one point of view that may be a more terrifying predicament than, as some modern novelists would seem to suggest, being condemned to meaninglessness. Responsibility may be abandoned if we are condemned to meaninglessness. Man's burden is to find meaning and to relate to it. From the evolutionary perspective we are also condemned to direction. Nothing remains the same. In the chain of continuity in our past, our forbears have been condemned to direction unwittingly; we, knowingly. If we choose no specific direction, our very drifting will be choice.

The reason that man is not still evolving physically to any pronounced degree is that he now not so much adapts to his environment as adapts the environment to himself. He has been so careless of his stewardship, so profligate in his use of the earth's resources, that the resulting pollution of air and water and earth threaten his continued well-being, if not his very existence. There are hopeful signs, however, that man has begun to face up to the implications of what is happening to his environment and the terrible consequences that will ensue for him and his children and his children's children if he does not at once set about a reversal of the pollution trend.

Happily, perhaps in the nick of time, he has recently come by a new "ecological sense" of the interpenetration and interdependence of every element and every animal within the environment, including himself. He knows now what should be done. Whether he will have the will and the energy to do it in time is still an open question. And this question is inseparable from the question of whether states will disarm progressively and sacrifice sovereignty to delegated international control, thus at once removing the continuing threat of nuclear warfare and releasing vast financial resources for the common war against pollution.

If by controlling and adapting his environment man has slowed down his continuing physical evolution, the pace of the evolution of his mind and conscience has been accelerated by the convergence of cultures and religions and the enormous productivity of scientific research. The new perspective on his existence brought to man by the camera's eye, relayed to television screens two hundred and fifty thousand miles away, has provoked sober reflection about the future of his own species. When one is closer to the moon's barren surface, the earth seems "good" in a more compelling and comprehensive way than ever before. And when one views the whole earth from outer space and observes that no national boundaries are distinguishable, the realization of Teilhard's prophecy seems more imminent: "The age of nations is past. The task before us, if we would not perish, is to build the earth."

Perhaps our celebration of the new day in which we live is chastened by some of these considerations. Man cannot now escape the conclusion that if he is to survive on this little spaceship he must forego mutiny. This is one of the occasions for celebration that our space age has brought us. Putting a man on the moon is the greatest exterior adventure ever undertaken by man, and it has happened at a time when millions could be simultaneously participant through sight and sound. We are witnesses! Who is not moved to celebrate the moment in mind and heart!

Now we know that if we could but harness the extraordinary potential of corporate research and computer techniques and apply it to poverty elimination, pollution control, food production and distribution, and the eradication of certain diseases, we should vastly improve the human condition on this planet. The major problems distressing and threatening the species are actually soluble, given the concern and the will, thanks to our age of scientific research. This knowledge is sufficient ground for celebration even in advance of the achievement.

Celebrating One's Own Being

We might call all these reflections objective grounds for celebration. But there are also subjective grounds, rising out of man's interior experience. There were critical moments in our development as children when we discovered or were provided revelation about what and who we were, at least in some degree. We were also given clues as to what we were meant to become, a sense of our own unique values. This was related, no doubt, to the values of our families, religious communities, social and cultural settings. Yet our individual values have a distinctive quality of their own. We are conscious that our values are not precisely those of others by whom we have been influenced. They are subtly different. What feeds a man's soul and uplifts his spirit is not at all the same as that which does so for his own brother, though they shared all the earliest experiences and influences as children. In our prayer of celebration, we need from time to time to reflect upon these values, and explore in imagination their possible source.

I am fully aware of the dangers of narcissism, but I am persuaded that relatively few human beings are afflicted by this malady. Infinitely more common is self-rejection, or at least insufficient love of self. All celebration that does not have its roots in self-affirmation is halfhearted, and riding for a fall. If we may conceive of God as a self-conscious being, would he not want most of all to celebrate his own unique existence! The mystery of our own existence is something with which we must come to terms first. Everything depends on whether, in the balance, we find our own existence a burden or an occasion for celebration.

The lyrics of popular songs occasionally reveal poetic and profound truths, however ephemeral and transient their expression. "I've got to be me" and "I did it my way" communicate an exultant self-affirmation I believe to be a valid religious experience. Provided it is offset by an equally profound sense of involvement and of identification with others, it is more to be commended than false humility and self-abasement. We are no more totally depraved than we are totally good. We have a right to celebrate our being in secret; and to begin our private prayer by exclaiming "Behold, my me is very good!" is therefore neither blasphemy nor a sin against the Holy Spirit. Not to do so may well be. We shall not be ashamed before God to affirm, "I'm glad to be me and not anyone else." Then we shall not overlook the deepest reason for celebration: my real me in some sense is God, *my* self and *the* self are one.

This being so, we shall put in sacred context wanting to do our own thing. This, too, is ultimately unselfish. It affords God his one present chance to do his thing through us as individuals in just this peculiar way. Each of us can do something as no other person in this world can do it, perhaps a number of things. Every man can think God's thoughts after him as no other man can, if he only will. But he can also do some little things for the common good as no other man can. What occasion for celebration is this!

And if he can enter into this mood of celebration and undertake the tasks of this day in this spirit, how much more confidently and creatively he shall move, not to say with how much more energy and staying power. Contemporary secular society accords importance to "doing your thing." But how much more richly endowed becomes the idea within the context of the divine milieu. On one level a man can draw legitimate satisfaction from doing his thing instead of chiding himself for not being able to do what others can do. But on a deeper level he can rejoice to do his thing, no matter how limited it may seem to others, because it is part of the divine economy and because the all-encompassing divine personality we call God will have to go unexpressed in this particular if he does not offer himself as a channel for such expression. What an occasion for celebration is that!

There are also the unexpected and unearned increments of pleasure and fulfillment that come to a man through the personality of others as he relates to them through his participation in their joy in doing their thing. Instead of yielding to the temptation of envy, he can celebrate this unique capacity they have. After all, why should he not rejoice? He should himself be the poorer if they did not do their thing. And anyway, it is not they but God-in-them who does what he can do only in them. Therefore, in himself and in them it is God he celebrates. Behold, God is indeed very good! It is not a burdensome duty, but the most natural and effortless pleasure to praise him and magnify him forever in this simple, daily ritual of recollection of occasions for celebration.

Celebrating Human-Heartedness

This privilege of celebration is one the Puritan did not allow himself. Therefore, his countenance remained characteristically dour. There are times to kneel at the wailing wall of contrition, and there are times to stand up and celebrate. We shall presently try to understand why a humble and contrite heart is not despised by the living God. Just now we are trying to interpret the importance he must attach to the celebration of the life he has given. Not to be a penitent is perhaps to place in jeopardy one's immortal soul. Not to be a celebrant is to forego the savoring of life eternal here and now! The first prompts one to turn from a wrong course with intent to lead a new life. The other enables one to sustain with relish his pursuit of the new life.

There are animals that appear to celebrate what they are in the form of abandoned enjoyment of their distinctive powers. We find that even a momentary vicarious identification does something to lift our spirits as well. Who has not found himself leaping from the water with the dolphins at play? Does some ancestral memory of our own water-borne life at an early stage stir within us? The effortless gliding of the eagle or hawk or sea gull and the sudden rise without apparent flutter of wing as the thermal upswing of air carries him aloft is a borrowed pleasure no previous existence could ever have afforded one of our own forebears. It's a direction we missed, and which we can but artificially emulate in our air-borne power vehicles. But a fellow feeling enables us to participate kinesthetically in a skill that will never be ours.

One almost wishes he could project into the consciousness of the proud thoroughbred the capacity to reflect on his own beauty when he walks, trots, canters, or gallops across the turf. We shall never ourselves bound into the air with the spring of an impala, surveying at a glance the distant scene which had been partially concealed by the high grass. But for the moment we delight in his celebration of his own peculiar skill. All this may seem one aspect of the classic "pathetic fallacy," but there is a perspective from which it would seem a deeper pathos and a more grievous fallacy not to enter vicariously into the celebration of life. Part of the bliss of an occasional prayer in solitude may even be dancing, as the poet taught us, with the golden daffodils.

And if we give scope in ourselves to this innocent practice of identification with other forms of life in the movements that seem, to our incurably anthropomorphic perspective, to reflect well-being, how much more should we celebrate our human estate! If animals were sentient, what would they respond to in man that seemed a dimension of life concerning which they would like to return the compliment? Is there in the wistful glance of some near cousin on the tree of life a trace of longing for a faculty which his divergent course of development precluded?

I think Confucius can help us here by identifying the most distinctive gift of man as "human-heartedness." What is human-heartedness? Perhaps it is primarily the grace of empathy which makes it possible to get inside the skin of others, to feel their sorrow and to share their joy as if these were one's own. Still more it may be the compassion that constrains one to bear the burdens of others because they *are* one's own as long as they beset others, to free others from the bondage that somehow engulfs us as well. Who is enslaved and I am not bound? Who hungers or thirsts and his plight does not give pause to my careless enjoyment of my present plenty? The motivation that will not give me rest until I have come to the rescue of some animal whose pain my resourceful response could relieve: human-heartedness. Were I some other animal, miraculously endowed with sentience and empathy, how I should rejoice to see a fellow creature possessed of such a power. How shall I then not celebrate in solitude so distinctive a gift that a kindly providence has bestowed upon me? How else shall I do honor to the God who has been patiently shaping and refining this quality for so many millennia in this one peculiar species amid his manifold creatures?

My very celebration of this quality I share only with

other men, as far as it is given me to know. Once it dawns on me how rare and precious a faculty it is, shall I not want to put it to practice in every conceivable opportunity this day shall afford, lest even in infinitesimal degree it begins to atrophy in me from want of use? This marvelous capacity is something new under the sun, on this planet at least. In the time-scale of evolution it happened only a moment ago. Also new under the sun will be my exercise of it in the relationships whose cultivation in my little half acre constitutes my peculiar responsibility. Wordsworth reminds us of this opportunity we might otherwise take too lightly when he speaks of

> that best part of any good man's
> life, his little, nameless, unremembered
> acts of kindness and of love.[2]

Part of this movement of prayer in solitude is to recollect quite specifically what we have observed in our reading, in another's speaking, or at first-hand experience, of such acts over the past twenty-four hours, lest they go altogether unremembered. And in remembering in secret we shall name them before God who will join us in rehearsing the ancient antiphonal response, rejoicing at his ever unfinished creation, "Behold, it is very good!" Human-heartedness. I must celebrate this newest marvel on the face of the earth if I would sharpen and ready this instrument in myself for the work it might perform in the next twenty-four hours, were I sufficiently sensitized.

Celebrants in the Eucharist of Life

This dreary world languishes for more celebrants. Am I not myself called to this ministry? Every day affords enough bread and wine for this secret and solitary eucharist: the bread that bears the nutrient for human-heartedness and the alchemy of human passion that can, touched by such a spirit, convert water into wine. I shall keep a wary eye open to the instant recognition of the precious ingredients. Whether my Mass be performed in some desert, real as in Teilhard's account of such an incident, or figurative as in some arid urban site where I may be called to live or work, the elements are never far to seek. It may be that my celebration must be discreetly restrained, lest I give offense to those who see nothing to celebrate. The anthem for the liturgy today may be pitched in a minor key, but I shall surely hear the plaintive melody none the less in the back of my mind if I keep my attention faithfully on the sacred task of administering this sacrament, whether there be any other in the congregation to share it or not.

It may be the uplifted face of a black child on a dusty road in the Transkei in South Africa, reflecting a trust and friendliness no white man there has any right to expect after such a protracted blight of his potential human-heartedness. But the expression reveals a light only some obscure manna from heaven could have nourished in that desert place. He offers me a wine—in that smile and in the tender outreach of the life behind that expression in the eyes—of a vintage no human skill could ever match. I may happen on his counterpart on a street in some unlikely urban jungle in America. Whatever the setting, I discover the altar has already been adorned and the candles lighted. The child himself is the acolyte who presents me with the elements for this particular Mass on the world. How shall I decline so imperious a demand to become for this moment the celebrant?

The elements may be conveyed in very different vessels. A cancer patient in some hospital may give evidence by the spirit in which he accepts his plight that he has inward access to what has been called the medicine of immortality, even when medical science has nothing more to offer and his body continues to waste away. His indomitable spirit transforms his very pain into a wine appropriate for the sacrifice. I observe with outward concern and offer whatever consolation genuine fellow feeling for the suffering of another can afford. At the same time there is a chamber in my mind which this event, outwardly merely a dread harbinger of death, remodels into a sanctuary, and the Mass, even though its form take on the special character of a requiem, goes forward unintended and unrehearsed. In the manner of another's dying I have been offered a quality of life that calls for celebration.

Someone once queried, "Ought we not to be kindly one to another, seeing that we are all down here dying together?" We are indeed dying men calling out to dying men. Some of us are apparently nearer death than others, but none can know the hour of his going. From the moment of our birth we have been destined for an event which only in the rarest of cases lies more than a hundred years hence, less than a moment away in the time-scale of an evolving universe. Teilhard de Chardin offered wise counsel to his fellow Catholics. They had always been told that the greatest good fortune would be to die while communicating. He pointed out that it would be a far better thing to learn to communicate while dying.

When occasionally we behold such a marvel in someone on the brink of death, or in others in the more protracted march of life whose destination is always, inevitably, death, the elements for the hidden celebration lie at hand. Once in a long while a saintly human being can join the angel of his own death in an extraordinary "concelebration," as when Teilhard, having written a bereaved friend *"tout ce qui arrive est adorable"* later confessed that he was himself engaged in trying to practice, stricken as he was with a heart attack, the specific implications of what he had in effect been preaching.

Whatever the occasion life may unexpectedly afford in the ensuing day, we shall be quicker to recognize it and to respond, if we practice the discipline of celebration in our daily private prayer. If we rehearse the distinctive inward attitude of mind and posture of spirit, we shall not be found wanting when some unlikely and unexpected encounter thrusts into our hands the chalice and the paten and challenges us to sing the doxology: "Praise God from whom all blessings flow. Praise Him all creatures here below. Praise Him above ye heavenly hosts. Praise Father, Son and Holy Ghost."

7

SENSING THE GRATUITOUS IN LIFE

CELEBRATING AND GIVING THANKS are not exactly the same thing. They are related, of course, and the same gesture may contain both attitudes. But there is a subtle difference. Therefore, prayer wisely makes room for both. Moreover, there is a certain logic in movement from celebration to thanksgiving.

The Interior Posture of Thanksgiving

Thanksgiving has to do with the inwardness of the way in which I receive and accept the good things of life. There is perhaps no more poignant line in *King Lear* than the cry: "How sharper than a serpent's tooth it is to have a thankless child!" It is not that any parent can demand gratitude from his child. To do so would be to preclude it, for gratitude can never be exacted. The best gifts are freely given. This is the meaning of "gratuitous." Nothing is expected in return, not even gratitude. Nevertheless, in the human relationship between father and child, in which so much that a good father does for his child is gratuitous, if there is no inward feeling of gratitude on the part of the child there is tragic loss.

It is not that the father needs the son's gratitude. It is rather that a certain sensibility is wanting in the son. He who is without gratitude remains a stranger to inward joy. "Yea, a *joyful* and a *pleasant* thing it is to give thanks." It is both a physical and a psychological impossibility to feel genuinely thankful and to wear a dour countenance at the same time.

At no other point is the distinction more clearly drawn between what we might call the secular and the religious man. The secular man accepts the bounty of life as his due. The religious man receives it as a gratuitous blessing, an unearned increment, a grace. The secular man reflects the attitude of a certain grasshopper in a Disney film whose theme song reflected the cavalier spirit: "Oh, the world owes me a living." The religious man is conscious of a debt of gratitude that can never be paid. Therefore, with Job, he cannot imagine any set of deprivations so severe as to transform him into an ungrateful child. "Though he slay me, yet will I trust him." The dear gift of life itself is such that he must be grateful no matter what may befall him. Else there is an internal displacement, more to be dreaded than any ill life can bring.

For the religious man the ultimate concern is to stay related to his God as a grateful child to his father, lest at some deep level of his being he cease to be himself. This interior posture of gratitude, moreover, makes all the difference. It bestows a quality of life that blesses not only him who possesses it, but all those whom his life touches at close range.

He is moved even to find ways of expressing daily gratitude for those very blessings he might be inclined to take for granted. He counts them over one by one as a miser hoards his jewels, and with the faithfulness of a Catholic reciting his rosary: "Thank you, O my God, this day, for such measure of health as I enjoy, for my work, my friends, my family, the little opportunities for service, the unexpected smile or glance of recognition, as of some shared secret, on the part of a chance passer-by." I sometimes think it is as simple as this: the religious man is the grateful man. He has a highly developed sense of the gratuitous in life and is motivated to guard it and to cultivate it as if his very life depended upon it. And indeed his deeper, richer life does depend upon it.

We commonly say of someone that he is an ungrateful wretch. The expression reflects not only our hostility against the secular spirit that robs life of one of its potentials, but our recognition that to be ungrateful is itself a wretched condition. It is a deprived, disadvantaged condition. It is a mean state, a falling far short of human capability.

The religious man has a nose for the gratuitous in life. He walks cheerfully over the earth, following its scent. It is a fragrance, a perfume, that goes undetected by the secular man. For the religious man it is a nosegay, never far to seek. It seems always coming to meet him from just around the corner. He is therefore constantly surprised by joy. He is fascinated not by the problem of evil (he thinks of evil as inevitable) but by the problem of good, whose omnipresence he finds totally unaccountable. When one has opportunity to study the countenance of a religious man one is struck by the play of a strange smile which does not always seem related to what is taking place outwardly, as if he were simultaneously perceiving inwardly another world of which others remained unaware. He has learned somehow to play a curious kind of solitaire which we can only call sensing the givenness or the gratuitous in life.

Teilhard de Chardin knew how to play this game. He tried to tell us about one of its marvelous rules: *"Tout ce qui arrive est adorable."* Now, on the face of it, that claim is perfectly absurd. How can I possibly believe that everything that happens is adorable or contains something that prompts to adoration? Yet, by some uncanny alchemy, all things do seem to work together for good to them that love the Lord, even many of the things we would have instinctively called bad. What is required in this wizardry of transformation would appear to be a childlike habit of receiving everything that comes as though it were offered by the hand of the Father. It is an ultimate trust, a total freedom from anxiety in any form.

After witnessing in utter amazement an expression of

kindly curiosity on the countenance of Teilhard as he suddenly encountered a poisonous snake coiled to strike him from the limb of a tree, the traveling companion on the journey through the jungle asked him why he was not afraid. Did he not realize how close to death he had come? "Yes, but there is nothing to fear. It would only have been a transformation." Apparently nothing happens that does not offer, however concealed to ordinary eyes, an occasion for adoration. Thanksgiving for the man of faith may be ceaseless because there is no conceivable set of circumstances that does not carry at its core a gratuitous grace for him who has eyes to see.

Transformation by Thanksgiving

To be able to sense the gratuitous transmutes the poor into bounteous givers. No state of poverty can deprive this enchanted man of whom we speak of the joy of bestowing as well as of receiving. He carries always one more gift in his invisible basket: gratitude itself. In cynicism the worldly are fond of recounting: "He who laughs last laughs best." This invincible idealist possesses a more useful secret: he who gives last gives best. That gift is invariably the gift of thanksgiving. It need not be spoken. The eye of him who is thankful reflects the glory of this buried treasure. But alas, the eye of another is a field that cannot be bought, however ready one might be on occasion to sell all he had to possess that one gift.

Gratitude is a tender and humble feeling. When a man experiences it, he is aware of a divine interior chemo-therapy that transmutes the commonplace water of his own vessel into the most intoxicating wine. He is made over. He is brought together. He is recreated. He is, in fact, a new man. And as long as its spirit is maintained within him he is relatively incapable of wrongdoing. Indeed he is not his own man. He belongs to another—the ineffable giver of all good things. It is not alone that others find him subtly different, more open, more responsive, more aware and receptive. It is also that he finds himself to be living on a different level, less vulnerable to hurt and consequent withdrawal, more pliable as an instrument for some form of service. This is a miracle he has not wrought. It is as if there were suddenly more of him. He can afford to lend more of himself without any sense of risk, and without asking any interest (self-interest). He can even lavishly give himself away, and is amazed to find that there is yet more to give than he had ever dreamed.

The joy issuing from the experience of genuine thanksgiving not only makes a man aware of the presence of this unfailing well, darkly hidden in the depths of his being and motivating him to give of himself, but compels him to give more generously of whatever he possesses of the things of this world of which his brother may have some need. He can no longer afford to be stingy or defensive of his possessions. Since he sees now that they have all come to him gratuitously, he can no longer feel that in any exclusive sense they are his. He can accept possessions without misery only on one ground: that he become a good steward of them, care for them, and keep them in good condition, and either give them away or share them as broadly as possible. He can only enjoy what he has on condition that he not be possessive of it and that he wisely bestow of his bounty upon others, sitting loose always to his own enjoyment of it. He may not rightly hold on to what he would not readily relinquish for the sake of the great giver should the latter ask it for a needy brother.

Douglas Steere speaks somewhere of happening upon a clearing after walking for some time in a dense forest. The clearing was a harrowed field, and striding across it was a sower, rhythmically reaching for seed and flinging it forth upon the waiting soil with a beautiful gesture that was at once expansive and profligate. Ever thus is the *great sower*. We ourselves are some of the seed grown to partial maturity. But we are also the soil, and if we are not barren we shall take into ourselves and warmly nourish what still is cast upon us in such great abundance. We are the gratuitous soil upon which gratuitous seed is still tossed with such abandon. And again quite gratuitously, we are called to be sowers. What responsibility is ours for the precious seed we are required to fling abroad with this same noble gesture in whatever little clearing we can manage in the dense forests that surround us! At the heart of the prayer of thanksgiving is a creaturely feeling toward the great Creator. Even while we are yet being "thrown" by the master potter, we are given our little wheels to learn some skill at shaping vessels that may hold water, perhaps even wine, for others.

Learning to sense the gratuitous precludes the covetous spirit. If my inward posture is one disposed to mar-

vel at my own bounty, how shall I look greedily upon
the possessions of another? Rather shall I learn little by
little to take pleasure in another's enjoyment of what he
has, provided always it is not marred by his misuse of it
or by unwarranted possessiveness.

Thanksgiving for the Unconscious

In an unforgettable parable Jesus taught us the unac-
ceptability of offering thanks for not being as other men
are. In our practice of thanksgiving there is no ground
for any sense of superiority, especially spiritual superiority, which is a particularly insidious form of snob-
bery. More natural perhaps, but no more acceptable, is
the tendency to express gratitude that we do not suffer
as other men do, with specific reference to known individuals or groups of individuals. Prompted by empathic
involvement in the suffering of a friend or loved one, a
man may instinctively want to thank God that he does
not have cancer. But note two dangers here. If his
thanksgiving today springs from his present freedom
from a condition he profoundly fears, what will his attitude be toward his God if on the morrow he discovers
he has contracted the dread disease? Moreover, the
spirit that prompts this kind of thanksgiving leaves out
of account the special blessings in adversity which the
friend may himself receive with genuine gratitude.

On the other hand, one may legitimately thank God
for the measure of health he enjoys this day, provided
he does not draw this kind of comparison, which must
be odious in God's sight, and provided he is growing in

that spirit that is inwardly preparing him to receive whatever may come his way as bearing in it an occasion for a new form of gratitude. There is no form of pain or suffering which, in the strange alchemy that makes all things work together for good to them that love the Lord, cannot be viewed from a new perspective, relating it to consequent changes in relationship and heretofore unexperienced quickenings of warmth and tenderness. It may therefore become, if not in and of itself, an occasion for thanksgiving, at least a contingency in part producing such an occasion.

The modern man who experiences himself as *duplex* rather than merely *simplex* (in Jung's sense) has discovered a vast new range for the expression of the spirit of gratitude. For most men, until very recently, the matter from dreams and fantasies presented to the conscious mind for reflection seemed more to be feared than welcomed. The one who spoke seemed more often adversary than friend, the message more often threatening than reassuring. At best, these figures, movements, images seemed eerie and unearthly, more provocation of shame and dread than trust. Hence we were inclined to drive them more deeply into the unconscious, to reject our dreams and fantasies as representing some kind of invasion from without by hostile spirits when we were least on guard. Somehow, they had to be repelled. This meant, in practice, deeper repression. In the meantime, a deep interior division in the self was fostered and unwittingly aggravated. Men were inclined to hide these strange, unfriendly visitations from those nearest to them and even to pretend to themselves that they made no sense and therefore bore no relation to reality.

When this willful banishment from conscious recognition and the studied refusal to confess their presence to others failed to banish them altogether there often grew a suspicion that one was different from others, perhaps even queer in an uncomfortable sense. Sometimes, because of their persistence, one feared the onset of insanity. To the feelings of guilt everyone bears, as a result of the inwardly accepted precepts and admonitions of his religious upbringing and cultural milieu, was added the imponderable weight of guilt for the presence of impulses of lust or fear or hate which found expression in dreams and fantasies.

Now that we know that the source of these imaginings is the unconscious, that it is an inescapable part of everyone's mental and spiritual life, that all men everywhere and at all times have been visited in much the same manner by similar spectres and images, we are able to look on this interior drama of encounter with some equanimity and objectivity. But far more. We have come to recognize through the insights of depth psychology that all of this activity at work in the unconscious, some of it floating into consciousness when remembered from dreams and directly encountered in fantasy, makes some kind of sense, whether trivial or of crucial importance, when one is helped to understand it.

Not only does it make sense, but a proper acceptance of its presence and an attentive attitude toward its message can help me realize a deeper integration as a person. These presences and voices are not enemies but veritably part of myself trying to communicate with my consciousness in order that I may become a whole person. They can be for me a blessing in disguise for they may well contain warning signals I could receive in no other way or answers to perplexities regarding my true identity and the course I should pursue vocationally.

When I realize that this is one place where, if I interpret it aright, I may hear the voice of God speaking to me, shall I not be thankful for what had once terrified me? Shall I not rejoice and give thanks for a contact with the Holy Spirit within, precisely at a point I had least thought to look for him? The images and the figures may still strike terror in my heart, and there will certainly be demons to be distinguished from the daimon. I must be very discriminating and get all the help available to me, but my new self-understanding as a result of listening to the messages from my own unconscious is something for which I can only be profoundly grateful.

Thanksgiving for New Vision of the World

If this is true of the world within that depth psychology has opened for me by revealing and interpreting the code in which the new language is spoken, it is also true of the exterior world of evolutionary continuity and ecological interpenetration. Whereas man had felt isolated from other living creatures and had a disturbing sense of standing over against the rest of nature, now he is in a position to see that he is very intimately related to all other creatures. He is closer to some on the tree of life than to others, to be sure, but he is born of the same process, stems from the same most primitive forms of life, and is dependent for his present existence upon a skein of threads so intricately interwoven that he shall never succeed in fully separating them for study and analysis. A student of paleontology, zoology, and anthropology—like Loren Eiseley—can enable us to stand with wonder and awe before both our differences from and our likenesses to other animals. We feel a kinship, even an identity with them such as we had never known before. We are now learning scientifically the basis for the mystics' experience of undifferentiated unity which has never before had such support in demonstrable fact.

The new evolutionary and ecological perspectives have provided us expanding horizons for experiencing the feeling of gratitude. It is not my parents alone who have given me my birth. The combination of genes which provided my potential endowment came from them. But the heritage of the peculiar set of genes that largely determined what I am runs back through evolution in an almost interminable sequence in which genes themselves have been evolving since the formation of life on this planet. Once men thought they owed their lives to God and to their parents. Now I know that I owe my birth to the whole process of evolution since its inception, and always in interaction with changing environment throughout that duration of biological space-time. And I owe my continuing life on a day-by-day basis to a delicate balance in the ecological environment of factors so complex and vast in number that even the new science has not scratched the surface of their extent and interaction with one another. How shall I not feel gratitude for the only partly fathomable continuity of the geologic ages and the mystery of the present interdependence of everything in the total environment when I owe my very existence to both of these realities?

With new eyes I shall begin to see other living creatures, the entire vegetable kingdom, the minerals, the water and air, which are equally vital in sustaining life. If I value my individuality, thank my God that I am me and that he has made his dwelling place in me as well as in all the rest of creation, must I not intuitively offer thanks from my heart for all that I spring from and intimately relate to and depend upon? From the perspective of the modern man whom we have identified, there is an infinite expansion of the operation of the gratuitous. All of it is grace. I have so much more to be thankful for than I had ever dreamed. It is no longer merely a matter of counting one's blessings that might be represented by a few beads on a string. I thank my God for the rising sun, the oxygen in the air, the remaining pure water of the earth's surface, the undefiled soil, the entire biosphere encircling the globe, and the superimposed noosphere insofar as this contains the potential of a great society to come, a milieu for the new man.

I shall now be able to learn from the mystics how to be fully at home in the universe. I must learn to trust the little intimations I have had that my condition of skin-encapsulation hides from me the deeper condition of interpenetration and unity with all that is. When I have thought, with Carl Jung, that I was not sure where my body ended and the rock on which I sat began, that was not madness, as I feared, but a perception of an important aspect of reality. I must fearlessly enter a cloud of unknowing that I may know much for the first time. I must unlearn the illusion of separation and learn the reality of interconnection. My first reaction to the infinite involvement by which I am now confronted may be to see it as an entanglement and to look impulsively for some escape. When I perceive there is no escape, I shall do well to accept my nothingness under God that I may begin to know my true significance. This will require an act of entrustment of myself not only to God but to his "good earth." This is the distinctive "leap of faith" required of the modern man. Then, perhaps, I shall be able to affirm with Teilhard my belief in "the value, the infallibility, the goodness of the World."

How shall I come by and cultivate in prayer this spirit of thanksgiving? I suppose that only God and his mysterious providence can produce in me the initial longing for this treasure. Ultimately the spirit of thanksgiving is itself a gratuitous gift, a grace. But once it has become for me a pearl of great price I can do something about it in my prayer in solitude. Even when I do not feel spontaneity in gratitude I can recollect the times of thanksgiving I have known. I can recover the memory of a happy occasion by gazing upon a pressed flower in a cherished book, a bird's feather hoarded in a wallet, a butterfly's wing once brought to me by the eager hand of a child. I can count the day's blessings one by one, even when my heavy heart cannot leap up. And if I turn as a child to my Father, trustingly, expectantly, he will himself blow upon the embers of my heart until they dance again in the full flame of gratitude. First I dutifully recount the things for which, when I was more myself, I could feel genuine gratitude. Putting aside any guilt for my emptiness I wait to be filled with the very gratitude I lack. At last, if I am patient enough, the greatest gift of all—a grateful heart—is once more given and I find myself whispering, "All things come of thee O Lord, and now of thine own do I give thee."

8

RISKING REJECTION
FOR DEEPER ACCEPTANCE

OUR ONLY ANALOGY for the divine-human encounter of prayer is the relationship between man and man, however inadequate this may seem. As friendship deepens, there is always the haunting suspicion that if the other really knew the depth and extent of one's own failures and misdeeds, he might lose respect and withdraw his friendship. That is why, as a warm human relationship develops, one experiences a longing to make confession, cautiously and partially at first. He wants to be more profoundly accepted as he really is, including his past, which is inevitably still a part of him. He finds himself prepared to risk rejection in order to win deeper acceptance.

If the risk is not taken, the relationship will seem

shallower than it might be, and will be plagued by moot questions and unintentional deceptions. Sometimes the gamble seems great, but the stakes are equally great. There is no escaping the validity of the dictum that all real life on the human level is meeting, and all richer life is meeting in depth. If human friendship would attain something of its inexhaustible potential, mutual confession, although gradual and indirect, is essential.

In that still richer relationship of a man and woman in love, in proportion to the passion to become one spirit as well as one flesh, there is the irresistible compulsion to share all secrets, past and present. Kierkegaard offered good counsel out of his own tragic experience. He held that the only person who should never marry is one incapable of living an open and revealed life toward the beloved. He himself had been unable to ask Regina to marry him because he could not bring himself to impart to her the secret his father had shared with him. Human love at its most intense provides the key to the need for confession in prayer. If I cannot feel at one with her whom I love, and unless I am prepared to make confession, how shall I come into the presence of my God without the compulsion to open my heart to him in a much more profound way?

The Need for a Human Confessor

Quite apart from the internal logic of human relationship as it moves toward more complete meeting and union, I have need to make confession to one other human being in order to keep my grip on my own identity. I need a human confessor, one who may represent to me the rest of humanity, against whom in my own "otherness" I am required to win my individuation, my identity, my integrity. One's identity, as Emily Dickinson reminded us, is a hound that all too easily slips its leash. Regular confession to one other human being provides another leash that serves to restrain this willful hound.

This person need not be a priest or professional confessor, of course. The confession may be quite informal. It may take place by correspondence with a trusted friend at some distance, and at irregular intervals. The one requirement is that the confessor should have demonstrated in some way that he is capable of seeing me as I see myself, particularly at the point of that elusive edge where I reach forward toward a cherished self-image with the infinite pathos that characterizes us all in this crucial, hidden drama. The ideal confessor I am commending here is not the traditional priest, the impassive, detached, holy man of God, who projects a general love for all mankind. This confessor must have a very particular love for this particular man or woman who risks rejection for deeper acceptance in his quest for sustained identity. We demand nothing less than that this confessor love the same me that I love most. Happy the man whose wife is also his friend and confessor!

The Threat of the Autonomous Complex

Why is it that I need a confessor in order to help me retain my identity and to pursue it forward into ever richer individuation and integrity? Part of the answer lies in the fact that the best that is in me will suffer atrophy if it does not find articulation and expression in human relationship. That is the positive reason, but there is a negative reason as well. There is in everyone the threat of at least incipient autonomous complexes. Here modern depth psychology has been particularly helpful in identifying the danger that lurks within.

Autonomous complexes are, of course, as varied in specific forms as men themselves, but there are certain recognizable general categories. An autonomous complex is the internal enemy in the identity struggle. It is not unlike a cancer in that for the health of the spirit it constitutes a foreign body with its own built-in diabolical capacity to expand like the cells of malignant tissue, drawing strength and sustenance away from the elusive identity of the person. It is potentially as death-dealing to integrity as is cancer to the body.

An autonomous complex may be formed about some compulsive ambition, some fear or aberration or violent hatred. It may take the form of a perverse attachment to some person which cannot be integrated with the other responsibilities and relationships of one's private and public life. It may arise from some untamed passion which in turn has its roots either in the abundance of sensual indulgence or its deprivation in infancy. Modern depth psychology helps us to understand how we can be afflicted in adult life by unconscious transferences upon specific individuals of a compulsive need either to recover or to make up for the want of sensual satisfactions in those first months of life.

A vainglorious ambition unrelated to talent or opportunity, an irrational fear or aberration, a persistent hostility, a dependence upon another that cannot be harmonized in the context of one's total life, all of these have a way of seizing upon the raw material of experience that every day provides, and of interpreting it, shaping it, utilizing it for their own purposes in total disregard of the potential for that constructive identity which is the health of the spirit.

It is the nature of the autonomous complex first to go into orbit on its own and gradually to demand that the true identity, the potential identity each man possesses as a child of God, go into orbit around it. This capitulation would be disaster: the disintegration of identity. The autonomous complex has a perverse identity of its own; that is why it is called autonomous. It is a complex because it forms a cluster of attitudes, dreams, and dependencies which have a pseudo-integration of their own. This cluster ever seeks to absorb the impinging territory of other commitments, however incompatible, in its insatiable drive to usurp the inner throne of selfhood.

A man needs a human confessor on two counts, therefore. He needs to confess to another, as clearly as possible, the best that is in him in order to keep it alive and flourishing. And he needs to confess to another not only specific wrongdoing but the mysterious core of the motivation for the worst wrongdoing, the sin against himself which the presence and growth of the autonomous complex constitutes. He needs to identify this complex, or it may be *these* complexes, incipient or well advanced, and to be helped to put up adequate defenses against their ever-threatening insurgency.

There is a special temptation for one who early wins the reputation among his friends and acquaintances of being a good man. He may indeed have very high aspirations that he may find it embarrassing to share with another. But if his self-image, partly shaped by his admirers, is such that he feels he cannot afford to share with another human being the dark side of his inner life in the form of real or potential autonomous complexes, he may be riding for a great fall.

As all the authentic saints have known, no man is so good that he has no need of a confessor, self-chosen from among his fellow men. Apart from this discipline, it is too easy to be self-deceived, to engage in rationalizing about the inner enemy until it amasses at last enough strength one day to assault the real identity. All men, without exception, need confessors. Woe unto that man who in his illusion of the grandeur of independence neglects to bind himself to another as he climbs the steep ascent!

Confession to God in Solitude

At the same time we must continue to acknowledge that no human confessor, no matter how much he loves us for our best self and remains patient with us in our struggle against the threatening complexes within, is sufficient for our deepest need. At our best we do have aspirations too elusive, too tentative and ephemeral, to confide. And we do have impulses too dark and shadowy to express clearly to another. To deal effectively with both of these we have no recourse but to resort to God in solitude. This ideal companion, who makes his home both in the innermost depths of the soul and beyond the reach of outer space, alone is capable of hearing and of comprehending the confession and of giving succor.

Of course, God, if we conceive of him as omniscient, already knows our condition before we make confession. If he is also all-loving, then this discipline of confessing to him what he already knows does not involve the risk of rejection which gives us pause in human encounter. Yet we are aware of a double risk in this more probing interior exposure in the sole presence of the great friend and confessor. As we look upon the incipient or advanced autonomous complex before and with him, we see and feel the extent of the conflict, the poignancy and the infinite sorrow involved in the threatened loss of identity. To be a saint is to achieve one's identity in God. That is why, as Leon Bloy poignantly put it: "There is only one sorrow, and that is— not to be saints." [1]

In the human confessor another concerned person wrestles with us for the preservation or the realization of the cherished identity. With the divine confessor there is the strange and awesome experience that the confessor is somehow bound up with this identity himself. In some sense he *is* the identity. This is why we must speak to God of our elusive aspirations and longings in the life of the spirit. We need not find words for them. We may simply offer them as we meditate upon them in prayer. In so meditating and offering in his presence we keep them alive and growing.

This is also why to engage in confession to God is to experience the *judgment* existentially. It is to see and to know the great gulf fixed between the autonomous complex and the true identity, and to experience the urgency, the infinitely portentous urgency, for decision and reform. Only here, making confession in the presence of almighty God, may we know what it is to be a penitent. As long as we can procrastinate and postpone this critical divine-human encounter we may conspire to evade the sense of urgency. But for the penitent, the man who sees the threat to his identity as the great companion-confessor sees it—who is himself an inescapable part of the identity—the present in confession is always the *eleventh hour*. This, Kierkegaard well knew. In *Purity of Heart Is to Will One Thing*, he insisted that the vocation of the religious man is to be a penitent. If this is a demanding vocation, there is a singular consolation: whereas with other vocations one's skill wanes as age advances, in this vocation we may continue to improve all the days of our lives, barring the onset of senility.

The first risk in the precious bane of confession before God in solitude is that one has to look at the great guilt, the guilt of furthering and fostering within, an intruding entity that can rob one of true identity. To yield to this enemy would be the ultimate sin, at once against oneself, one's neighbor, and one's God. Against oneself because there is no sin greater than to have forfeited one's chance to be himself, to realize his potential identity. Against his neighbor because, in losing his identity, a man surrenders all possibility of serving his fellows as he might and becomes an insufferable burden upon those whose burdens he might have made lighter. Against God, above all, because God bestowed upon him the priceless gift of his potential identity, and he persists in blocking the only opportunity God has ever had, or will ever have, of projecting his own identity in just this form into his creation.

The second risk he runs is that once he sees the truth of this revealed dichotomy under the relentless gaze of the companion-confessor, who is also the adversary of all that is inimical to the true identity, he is condemned to the unceasing toil of willing and striving to become himself for the sake of God. In making confession to God he does not risk rejection; he risks recognition of the only judgment that matters, and the consequent demand for interior reform.

If these are the risks he runs, there is also the blessed promise of an acceptance more profound, more comforting, and more reconciling and restoring than the most exalted and long-suffering human love can offer. If this seems a paradox, it is because we are speaking the language of religion which, as we have said, always and inevitably takes the form of paradox. Only he who is ultimate demand is also in position to offer final succor. Our comfort and consolation derive from the realization that he has made us as we are. Therefore, as long as we importune, he will not abandon us. He should thereby cease to be himself, and this is unthinkable. He has not only made us as we are, that is, the kind of being who can harbor autonomous complexes, but he has made us for himself, indeed as some kind of extension of himself into his continuing creation. This is the source of our restlessness. We are restless until we find our rest in discovering and maintaining our true identity for him and in him.

The Blessing of Forgiveness

In this practice of confession to God in solitude we are granted forgiveness for all our past failures and sins. God is not only prepared to forgive but even to forget our sins, a faculty others against whom we have sinned do not possess. But we are required also to accept this forgiveness and to forgive ourselves. Our dreams are reliable informants of those sins for which we have not yet forgiven ourselves. We do well to be attentive in this way to what is still experienced on the unconscious level when we may have succeeded in banishing it from the conscious. For self-forgiveness to take place in a deep-going way it may be necessary to confess the same sin and to accept forgiveness for it every day for many years, until the unconscious itself reassures us that the healing has been accomplished. The psychological truth demonstrated by Alcoholics Anonymous is applicable here: Receive and embrace daily the offered forgiveness and live *into* the forgiven life for the next twenty-four hours.

Assured of God's forgiveness in the depths of the inner man, confirmed and sealed by the act of self-forgiveness, we must be very wary of accepting any element of continuing shame which a cruel society may wish to impose for some past act which it condemns. There are those who would debilitate us by inflicting upon us an unending sense of shame. Even the Church of Christ has often revealed itself to be far less forgiving than its God. We are required by the God who forgives and forgets to put aside the shame with which society, and even segments of the Church, might want to shackle us, and to walk free in his sight in whom alone judgment rests, always remembering, of course, that he who would be forgiven much must also forgive much in his fellows.

Finally, in the practice of confession in solitude before God, we are granted an ineffable grace if we but open up and expose ourselves to receive it. We may enter a state where earthly standards of right and wrong are transcended in a sense of union with the godhead that lies beyond, before, and after our Judaeo-Christian God of righteousness. The mystery of this blessing is hinted at in the biblical insight that God is of too pure mind to behold iniquity. As the early myth put it, because we have eaten of the fruit of the tree of the knowledge of good and evil, in our human encounter we are condemned to a lifelong struggle between good and evil, even within. In our prayer of confession we may happen upon a secret, metaphorical re-entrance into the Garden of Eden where we may find rest, even if only momentarily, before we are required to renew the struggle.

9

STRIVING TO BE
A MAN FOR OTHERS

No traditional form of prayer stands in greater need of change and expansion than what has been known as intercession. Whole communities of monastics have been dedicated to the practice of interceding before God on behalf of all mankind. The motivation for this prodigious labor of prayer, with such concentration for such protracted hours, is unimpeachable. And I am persuaded that in the divine economy this labor has not been in vain, but has been an important factor in the ecology of human existence. Had not some men and women devoted their lives to intercessory prayer, the critical quotient of mutual concern in the family of man may well have been lowered to the vanishing point in a given era at a given place. Nevertheless, our images and implied metaphors as to what is or should be taking place in this particular form of prayer need radical revision and updating to allow scope for our expanding insights into the nature of man and community.

The predominant image of God projected by classical intercession was that of an austere monarch who could be importuned by some of his subjects to transform the condition of others. The God to whom intercession was addressed was generally conceived as being altogether transcendent. Through the vicarious supplication of some men on behalf of others, he could be induced to take special action that apparently might not have occurred to him otherwise, or would, at any rate, not have come to pass without such intervention. If this God, so narrowly conceived by so many for so long, is now dead for many of our contemporaries, I for one find it hard to mourn the loss. What I do passionately long for on their behalf is the resurrection of a new and greater God in whose presence they can carry forward and express the very valid compassion and concern that motivated the former practice.

Beginning with the Immanence of God

The first step in any effective contemporary prayer for others is to become clear about the immanence of God without denying the transcendence. God is as much present in me and in those for whom I undertake to pray as he is any place else in the universe he has created. More than this, he is trying to express himself in them as well as in me. Even before we undertake the labor of love involved in this prayer, we have this all-but-unbelievable reality working for us. Already, in process and progress, there is this vital force awaiting opportunity to break through in fresh, creative manifestations. God is in my friend for whom I pray, striving to become himself in this unique person, even as he awaits liberation in me.

This is not to deny that God also retains his transcendent dimension. Of course, he is also, and at the same time, *infinitely other* and infinitely remote from this particular manifestation of his presence. But the important point we are making here is that the transcendent God has a present diaphany here in this man for whom I pray, if I but have the eyes of faith with which to see him. I use the word diaphany here as Teilhard uses it when he speaks of the "diaphany of the divine at the heart of a universe on fire." If so great a mystic could perceive the diaphany even in matter itself, how much more ought we to train ourselves to see it in that matter which is a man. I am not to confuse my friend with God. But I am required to try unceasingly to see that of God in him. When I do, if I am willing to devote time and imagination and energy, I may be used by God as an instrument to help him achieve a minor *epiphany* in that man—that is, an outward manifestation as well as an inward one, visible only to the eye of faith.

Identifying Through Role-playing

As has been true in our attempt to reinterpret in order to revitalize other classic forms of prayer, we must once more turn for analogy to new insights into the dynamics of human relationship in order to expand our vision of the divine-human relationship. In the last two decades we have learned a great deal from experimentation with group dynamics in the various forms of sensitivity training in brief but intense, as well as in marathon, encounters. Inspired by the depth-psychological insights of modern psychiatry, the pioneering work was undertaken by secular groups, initially at Bethel, Maine. Now the process has burgeoned to the point that it has become one of the pseudo-religions of our time, with its own ashrams and retreat houses, such as that of the Esalen Institute, proclaiming the "good news" of salvation in its own terms, creating its own rituals and dogmas.

What the Church has recognized, however, in its prompt assimilation and adaptation of the techniques, is that the purveyors of the new religion are in possession of some exciting new insights that can indeed release creative energies while enabling the individual to understand and to accept himself. These techniques, pursued under the guidance of wise and sensitive men and women, have enabled many persons to know and to confront the truth about themselves in areas in which they had long been unperceptive or self-deceived. In an unexpected way, from an unanticipated source, the ancient prophecy has been fulfilled: "Ye shall know the truth and the truth shall make you free." Knowing the truth about oneself certainly does bring the opportunity for new freedom.

Unhappily, the new techniques and processes are by

no means universally effective for good. There are many casualties as well as examples of notable success. Men may learn a great deal about themselves without being provided a means of integration. Forces may be released that can be more destructive than when repressed. The new techniques may be used by unscrupulous group leaders for the purpose of manipulation, to their personal ends, both of individuals and groups. We are familiar with the form of vivisection that involves surgical experimentation with live animals for the sake of the advancement of medical knowledge to be applied to the improvement of the health of mankind. The new encounter process makes available to some a form of vivisection upon the living tissues of feeling and reflection which has inherent dangers. There are individuals who derive personal excitement and pleasure from the process without due regard for and insight into the dangers into which they may be bringing others. The process for some may become a pursuit of pleasure so insatiable that they live from one such experience to another, unconsciously demanding that the next one be more exciting than the last.

Once one has acknowledged the dangers and the limitations, however, and provided that a genuine reverence for the infinite value of the individual person is scrupulously maintained, one can learn a good deal from those techniques that is applicable to the practice of intercessory prayer. I am thinking particularly of identification and role-playing. Unlike many of our forebears in the Church, we must assume that God is already on the side of the person for whom we pray, willing his health and vitality and fulfillment, and doing what he can to those ends.

The main purpose in our prayer becomes, then, making available to those purposes our own psychic energy and resourcefulness. In praying for others my primary objective must be to become for God, in relation to the person for whom I pray, as a man's right hand is to a man. That is to say, I want to become an instrument available and effective for God's use. This requires an imaginative entering into the person and life of my friend: identification and role-playing. I want to try to stand where he stands, feel what he feels, think his thoughts after him, experience his characteristic reactions. If he is sick, I want vicariously to feel the intensity of his pain. We do not know the limits of psychological interpenetration and substitutionary involvement. Until we do, and are proven mistaken, I am prepared to follow my instinct that I can take some of this pain upon myself, thus relieving him to some extent.

Charles Williams in *Descent Into Hell* [1] bears witness to what he calls the doctrine of substituted love. A young woman, Pauline, is driven to distraction by the increasingly recurring experience that another person she fears is approaching her on the street when no one else is present. She cannot disabuse her mind of the conviction that this other person is somehow herself, and is overcome with fear of possible direct confrontation. They never quite meet but the dread persists that sooner or later they will. Pauline finally brings herself to tell the poet-playwright, Peter Stanhope (whom she greatly admires), of this aberration. Instead of making fun of her, or telling her that she is deluded, he takes her with full seriousness and finally convinces her that the next time the figure appears she is to remember that he, Peter, will take the fear on himself, thus freeing her to meet the figure without anxiety. She obeys and the figure does not even appear. I believe that Williams is here imparting through fiction a spiritual truth, relating, as the character Peter Stanhope insists, to what Jesus meant by bearing one another's burdens. Where there is love and trust, another's burden may, at least in part, be lifted and carried, whether it be fear or pain or anger.

I can also identify with the resources for recovery in another and add the mite of my will and energy toward a more vigorous flow of these resources. I can meditate purposefully upon the various energies and skills available in doctors and nurses attending him and the wonders of chemical, physical, and surgical therapy. Perhaps I shall be able to provide an extension of these resources in some way if I become sensitive to their rhythm and harmony. Where, to the best of medical knowledge, there is no chance for recovery, I will recognize that the need of the patient is for inner acceptance insofar as he is conscious of his approaching death, not in the spirit of hopeless resignation but of open, fearless fascination and trust. My energies will be devoted to thinking and feeling my way into such an attitude, borrowing, as far as I may, his patterns of thought and feeling as I know them. This is, of course, a working with him, a deep-going identification with him in his predicament, a role-playing on his behalf. I believe God can use this discipline, this offering made simultaneously to him and to my friend.

What Intercessory Prayer Accomplishes

One thing is quite obvious: in the process of intercessory prayer I become a more sensitive, more concerned, more responsible human being. Something happens to *me* that I *know* is *good*. I am for the moment moving in the direction of becoming a better person. And everybody in any way dependent upon me is so far served. And I believe something else is happening, less obvious but none the less real. I believe my prayer works both *for* God and *for* this person. It *does* something. I don't want to try to say what it does, because I don't understand it. And anyway it seems to me important that I not fix in my mind anything I would acknowledge as an answer to my prayer. As I must commit into God's keeping my friend and his condition, I must commit into his keeping my own partial and blundering efforts on his behalf. But I do feel confident that, in a world in which physical energies like light and sound and color and electrical charges can move invisibly and interconnect matter in space, spiritual energies must also interconnect and interpenetrate in some way as yet unknown. Therefore, in my prayer for my friend I provide God an additional channel for the movement of his energies to my friend. I believe my prayer on his behalf does something good for my friend, whether he recovers or dies.

Here I am moved to interject the conviction that it is wrong and even cruel to disseminate the idea that if someone is sick it is always because he is not right with God, and that the object of prayer must be to discover the obstacle in him and exorcise it. Of course it is true that the unity of body, mind, and spirit is such that in many individual cases physical illness is psychosomatic, and the one thing needed is setting right some interior attitude of hate or fear or wrong dependency. This truth is so often reiterated in our time that it can almost go without saying. Jesus could heal the paralytic because he knew intuitively where the source of the illness lay: in guilt. But to put all physical or psychological illness in this category is a tragic mistake. Just because we are psychosomatic beings, physical illness produces unhappy psychological states, and we must allow for the fact that for the individual, and so indirectly for his friends, sickness, even protracted suffering, can miraculously be put to some good end. All things, including sickness and suffering, *can* work together for good to them that love the Lord.

We have been speaking of prayer for those who are afflicted, temporarily or permanently, or who may be in terminal illness. However, the great weight of our intercessory prayer on a day-by-day basis will be directed toward the development or fulfillment of those we love or for whom we have special responsibility. Here again identification and imaginative, creative role-playing are the important resources. As in sensitivity training and encounter groups, the attention is focused upon what makes another tick, as we say, upon his feelings, values, and needs, conscious and otherwise, so that we can come to understand him from within and role-play his responses to given situations. Has not profound intercessory prayer always been, and does it not remain today, the most effective form of sensitivity training?

In solitude we concentrate upon *becoming,* for the time, our friend, thinking his thoughts after him, feeling his emotions, experiencing his needs. In proportion as the particular relationship indicates, we will endeavor to see ourselves as he sees us, no matter how difficult this may be, in order that we may relate more creatively to him. This is one of the objectives of group dynamics. Here, in prayer, there is an important difference, an added dimension of incalculable significance. One tries to see his friend under the aspect of eternity as well as in certain specific situations and relationships. One tries to comprehend something of his infinite value before God, what he might become in God and what God might become in him.

There is in this friend the point at which his real self and the Self are one. This is where he really lives, now, and in some sense, forever. This is the point of deepest connection between him and God, but also between him and me. This is where all three of us are one. That is why my concern, my labor of concentration, count for him. I really live in him, and he in me, and both of us in God. I will try honestly to assess and to *experience* his strengths and his weaknesses, his aspirations and his besetting temptations, as far as it is given me to know these. I will weigh his resources and I will role-play both what he does with them and what he might do with them with better self-knowledge and a little more motivation.

For this brief span of time I am living his life vicariously. My caring for him is a form of energy taking the shape of longing for his growth at just this or that specific point which I conceive to be his present need. I vividly imagine a changed attitude, a released fear or dependency, a setting free from some habitual block in him. I offer this effort to God for him. But I must all the while recognize that what I want for him may not be what God wants, or what is best for his ultimate growth in God's sight. Nevertheless, as long as I remain sensitive to the possibilities of unworthy or irrelevant projections on my part, what I am doing can help in some way. I feel sure of it, as I feel sure I am helped by those who pray unselfishly for me.

Praying for One's Enemies

In this brief treatment we must forego consideration of the many questions that arise with regard to the efficacy of intercessory prayer. The questions and most of the classical responses are familiar to the thoughtful reader. We must, however, apply the general points we have been making to the practice of prayer for our enemies. I am thinking now not of vast, amorphous, stereotyped, national enemies. I am referring to specific persons who rub us the wrong way, who hurt or offend or injure us in some way, in a word, those persons whom we find it hard to take or can't stand, but with whom we must come into more or less close contact in the context of our present lives.

I am thinking of those persons who, were we to be locked up with them in one room throughout all eternity in the present state of our relationship, would constitute for us some kind of hell, the kind of hell three people create for each other in Jean Paul Sartre's *No Exit,* for example. We should all have to admit that our most intense psychological suffering derives from a relationship, or a complex of relationships, in which the demands and counter-demands, the dependencies and unfulfilled needs, the ambivalences of love-hate feelings producing, alternately or simultaneously, rage and guilt, are such that there would appear to be no exit. But with the help of active and creative intercessory prayer there *is* the possibility of an exit. Not by opting or "copping" out of responsibility, not by running away or withdrawing, but by trying imaginatively to discover and to identify what it is in us that enables that other or those others, taken one by one, to constitute some kind of hell for us. We can only change them by changing something in ourselves.

The focus of the role-play must be to see ourselves as they see us in order that we may come to know what it is we think or do or say or feel which threatens or angers or unnerves them. Once we are reasonably sure what it is, effectual intercessory prayer becomes petitionary prayer. We wrestle with the angel of the Lord until he works some blessed change in us that robs our adversary of his ability to produce any kind of hell for us. That is one deprivation in the case of another that we are justified in assuming responsibility for. Sartre's drama, with the playwright's license and in the spirit of nihilistic existentialism, leaves the victims in hell. We are grateful to him for holding so faithful a mirror to that which can and does constitute present confinement in hell. But we have been shown a more excellent way, an escape hatch, an *exit*. With the aid of modern depth-psychological insights, combined with relentless self-analysis and earnest pleading before the Lord, we may identify our own projections, compulsions, and transferences that afford the adversary his power to put us in hell. One by one, with God's grace, we can remove or at least exercise control over these. In freeing ourselves we also free our enemy from exercising a power that could have brought him no benefit. At last we may begin to be able to pray for him as for those for whom we *care*.

Prayer on Behalf of the World

Finally, what of the vast company who stand in desperate need, at home and abroad? Our prayers cannot encompass the world, save in the most general forms. And the more generalized they are, as in all human endeavor, the least personally effective they are. As we have special responsibility to pray for those with whom our lives come into daily contact in family relationships or work or service, so we have special responsibility to those suffering from some form of deprivation we are in a position to alleviate by some specific personal or social action, or both. Is it racial discrimination, economic, educational, or medical deprivation? Again the work of intercessory prayer must take the shape first of active, imaginative—yes, dramatic—identification in depth, so that one thinks and feels his way into the condition of those for whom one prays. Feel the rejection, know the anguish of the want, experience the suffering so that it becomes one's own. Then dwell with all the imagination and resourcefulness of which one is capable on what an aroused society might do to right the wrong, to relieve the pain, to transform itself in such a way as to prevent the continuation of such human waste.

At last it must always come down to what one person, namely myself, in proportion to other legitimate demands, interests, and responsibilities, can do about it. I can at least do thus and so, reform my own thinking and feeling and acting here and here and here. I can see this person, write that letter, vote in this way, engage in such-and-such specific action including, on occasion, nonviolent direct action, even civil disobedience. I can identify and support those groups which seem to me to be making constructive contribution. I can translate my concern into personal transformation and direct action, always remembering that faithful intercessory prayer at once keeps alive and deepens the concern, while it leads to openings that show me what I can do about it today, tomorrow, and the day following.

10

WORKING FOR

INTERIOR WHOLENESS

IN THE FORM of prayer that has been called petition there is a similar need for radical change of perspective on the human posture in relation to God and on the focus of anticipation. In such prayer we do not abandon the notion of God's transcendence. I stand in need of what he alone can give. I remain a petitioner with respect to God. He is the Other, the totally Other, as over against my "me" in process of becoming. At the same time, and this is the point much of the teaching of the Church has neglected, God is also immanent. I am made in the image of God. He lives in me. My body is the temple of his Holy Spirit. His very self is so united with my self at its core that I am unable to distinguish between them. My experience in moments of insight and revelation is that they are one.

What I am saying, of course, may sound illogical and inconsistent. But religion demands that we faithfully witness to experience even when our attempt to describe it must be judged, from the rational point of view, illogical and inconsistent. Perhaps the proper word for it is *paradox,* which in this case represents a coincidence of opposites, both of which are true to experience. The problem has been that in its attempt to be logical the Church has neglected a valid aspect of experience.

The New Complexity of Petitionary Prayer

In this chapter we are to see what a strange position a man finds himself in when he engages in petitionary prayer. As a creature he stands in need of physical nourishment and shelter, the means for which have already been provided by his Creator, else he should never have arrived through the long process of evolution, nor now be alive for that matter. Yet, in our modern civilization he is dependent not only upon his own will to live, to forage for food and to look for or to create shelter, but also upon a vast complex of factors involving the interior attitudes of others and exterior social, economic, and political conditions. So inescapably interrelated is everything in this life that every form of prayer involves every other form, at least by implication.

In bringing his petition for daily bread before almighty God, a man is also obliged to recognize that the prayer can only be answered through a favorable operation of many intricate and interlocking processes in society. So the simplest petition demands intercession as well. No need is greater or more basic than that for food and drink and shelter. A man may neglect prayer for these unless or until he is desperate. Then he finds himself praying for them whether he intends to do so or not. He may not have understood what the prayer of petition (in the Lord's Prayer, for example) really is until that moment.

The Centrality of Identity

But man does not live by bread alone. He is a highly sophisticated animal with many other needs which must be met if his life is to carry with it any inner sense of fulfillment. Both for economic reasons, in order to be able to earn a living, and for psychological reasons, in order to feel needed and appreciated by his fellows, he must find a vocation in which his talents can be put to work for his own benefit and that of others. In order to find and to pursue a vocation he needs an education of some kind. This in turn costs money and requires the labor of good teachers. He needs also access to a doctor when he is sick, and to medical counsel in order to stay well through preventive medicine. He needs recreation and rest, a social life, and some measure of solitude.

For genuine fulfillment as a person, he needs to be loved by others and to be able to give love in return.

Moreover, he needs to be loved not for anything he can do for others but, in the last analysis, for what he is, inside: the special little bundle of hopes and dreams that make him the unique individual he is. And, in order that this richest fulfillment may be realized, he needs to discover and to maintain his own identity. The dignity of being a man, as distinct from any other animal, exacts this responsibility: to discover who one is and who one would become.

Here we arrive at the most important functions of the prayer of petition: an opportunity to discover both who one is and who one would become in one's quest for identity and integrity, and to secure a leverage for realization of this greatest human fulfillment. We have said that in petitionary prayer man is in a strange position. And so he is. In addition to the inevitability of appealing to the great Other for the continuance of the necessities of life, he finds that this same Other, to whom he must also appeal for the greatest blessings of selfhood and individuation, resides in some mysterious way in the depths of his own being.

On the one hand God has put this desire for selfhood in him, and on the other he has already sown the seed that may flower into identity and integrity. Not only that; in some unfathomable way which the mystics bear witness to, but cannot explain, this very other *is* this identity itself at its source and spring. God is at once the Other and the very Self of my self. You are saying now: "He is speaking in riddles; what he is saying doesn't make sense." And you are quite right. I am speaking of a riddle that has never been solved. But what I am saying, while it may not seem to make sense, does make life, the life that is religion.

If, then, I am to move beyond the shallows of petitioning for food and shelter and a reasonable share of this earth's goods into the deeps where I must seek to know and to become myself, I find I am addressing my God in a different posture. Of course my becoming myself in the end depends upon the timely convergence of many exterior factors, just as does the attainment of the material goods I require: opportunities, response from my fellows, an infinite variety of factors. But the most important single factor in my becoming fully myself is the elusive and subtle process of assimilation, reflection, evaluation, and integration that takes place in the depths of my being.

In the prayer of petition I am both witness to and an active, purposeful, participant in the process. I both meditate upon what God has done and is doing in me and study what I must now do and think and be if I am to become myself. Once again I appeal to the Other, who is also within, for help. Here we need to bring to mind again that penetrating observation of P. T. Forsyth[1] to the effect that prayer (especially, we would add, petitionary prayer) is overhearing the converse between the Father and the Son in the depths of one's own being. The Father and the Son are both in me. The self is the Father and the self is the Son and, far enough in and deep enough down and high enough up, they are both one. So, as petitionary prayer moves on this level, I find myself addressing primarily the God within, listening with my inner ear to him who is closer to me than I am to myself.

But now we must make another very important point. Insofar as God is the Other, even within me, I experience him as the great lover of my own soul. I can love myself not merely because he made me as I am, but because he *is* me as I am, at least in germ and by promise. This is the open secret the mystics have imparted, the ineffable mystery at the heart of human experience.

Love Is Not Blind

The consummation of this union between my self and the Self, God, I may experience only once or twice in a lifetime. But even if I have had only the slightest approximation to it, have stood, as it were, only on the threshold of experiencing it, I shall never be allowed to forget it. Henceforth, all my reflection upon the meaning of life must come around to this point and start again from here. (I hope that my reader will be able to confirm here, out of his own experience, what I can only indirectly allude to.) At other times the relationship to God must take an "I-Thou" form, even when it is inward. And this I-Thou relationship is, and must evermore become, the great love relationship of a man's life. All other loves must be experienced within this context, and made to conform to its demands.

Once again we must revert to analogies on the level of human relationships. It is commonly said that love is blind. Nothing could be farther from the truth. Always allowing for the incurable ambivalences in human nature which juxtapose love and hate as alternating and variable ingredients in every deep-going relationship, the person who truly loves another becomes thereby more discerning of that other's faults. Only the shallowest and the most fleeting love is blind. The weaknesses and failures of the beloved are observed and known most poignantly of all by the lover. Just because the beauty, realized and potential, is perceived and valued more by the lover than by all others, the weaknesses and failures seem the more tragic.

Anyone who has ever been in love (and is that not, at least in some degree, nearly everyone who reads this?) knows this truth of which I speak. The secret of a great lover is that he has not merely responded affirmatively to exterior comeliness; he has penetrated the inner citadel and has proclaimed as beautiful that fragile vision which the beloved has of what she would like to be. This above all else about her he confirms as beautiful! This he embraces with all the passion of which he is capable; he would give, he fancies, his very life in its defense. He has his own vision of what this is. He could not reproduce it in words or painting or even music. Nevertheless, he experiences it. Because he does—and this is really why he has captured, taken by storm, his beloved—she is able to value herself more than before. She has received the sacrament of confirmation.

And here's another mystery. One cannot be sure how much the vision that is confirmed was there already, intact, and how much it is created by the lover. The most probable truth is that it is a combination of both. As we noted in an earlier chapter, Mrs. Herman is accurate in suggesting that we are in some sense created by our friends. How much more, then, by a lover whose capacity for friendship is infinitely extended!

Now, of course, there is always the inherent danger that the lover may project upon the beloved an image of herself that does not correspond with her own potential, but is rather a mirror image, or a projection of himself or of some unrecognized need of his own. This can lead only to terrible frustration and ultimate breakdown of the relationship. Genuine self-love does not need to make such projections, and true love for another has both the capacity to discern what is there and to resist the temptation to impose an image that might seem to answer the need of the lover but, in fact, does violence to the identity of the beloved. Given these precautions and reservations, I think it is fair to say that, on the human level, nothing is more helpful in achieving identity than falling deeply and abidingly in love, unless it be the discovery of genuine vocation.

This is the inward desire of the man who falls in love: "I want to be me for her." The drive to realize identity has been given new and unexpected support from another, it may be even an unanticipated direction of quest. He sees himself in a new light, as a new man. The self-image changes. The self-love deepens through this convincing confirmation of being lovable. If the new vision is viable in the sense that it is one that can be lived up to in practice so that there is not too great a distance between the aspiration and the realization, then there has been a significant new turning, and there follows a new impulse of energy for the pursuit of identity. What we have been describing can of course be true in varying degree of any human relationship whose balance is positive and creative. I have chosen to speak of the ongoing love between a man and a woman because I believe that of all human relationships it is the most potent, generative impetus to the identity quest.

The Love Only God Can Give

But if we ask this love relationship to suffice for what might be the love of a man or a woman for God, then we at once are guilty of idolatry and simply place upon this form of love a burden it is not capable of bearing. In addition we severely inhibit the progress in depth that might be made in the pursuit of identity to its ultimate goal of individuation and integrity. Our human capacity to love and to be loved is greater than can be satisfied by any other man or woman in the world. It simply isn't fair to ask any person, however initially willing until the frustrations mount, to give us the kind of love our inward nature both demands and responds to. Only God can do this. And what a merciful lightening of an unbearable load when a man and woman place their love for each other within the context of this greater love each has for his God! Then the wonders of what human love can do, in tender and unexpected response and undeserved concern and loyalty, can be received with celebration and gratitude because they are not required.

The incurable loneliness of which we complain so

much even in a happy marriage is a good thing. Instead of driving us to seek satisfaction in some other relationship, always a frantic and ultimately futile pursuit, it is intended to direct us toward our solitary relationship to God, who alone can give the love we need and receive what we need to give.

Does this seem to you too much like the child who creates his own imaginary companion out of his need? I won't deny that it is like that. The great companion, the great lover of my soul, may well be my own creation, out of my own need. That is why in some sense my God remains different from your God. But something or someone projected this need into me all the way up through evolution, and at the same time the strange capacity to imagine the kind of person, God, who could satisfy the need. It may, indeed, all be a figment of my imagination. I can only say that as I develop the practice and allow my conception of the companion to grow by refinement in response to reflection upon the nature of the God of Abraham and the God of Isaac and the God of Jacob—and of Moses and David and Jesus, but also of Buddha and Lao-Tse and Gandhi and Martin Luther King and other great contemporaries—my intimations and assurances of this objective existence grow and I find my own life richer and more meaningful.

I must testify to the reality of this love relationship as the richest and deepest fulfillment of my life. Of course it is demanding and painful. But is not all human love so? As the great desire of the lover is to become for her sake the self he has discovered in and through the beloved, so this love relationship demands of me that I become myself for the sake of my God. But this demand is one with my deepest desire. Moreover, this ultimate demand, as we must keep remembering, springs from him who is also my final succor. He who asks so much of me not only forgives my persistent failure to be myself but provides me with the strength, as often as I fall, to pick myself up and to try again, with the wisdom to know the next step forward and the motivation to take it.

Wanting to Be Me for His Sake

This "wanting to be me for his sake" I take to be an authentic religious experience. Many human relationships, especially falling and remaining in love with one person, can be very helpful. But only the love relationship with God can make me gradually both my own man and his man. The only person capable of being completely unselfish in his vision of what I am to become is God himself. He asks only that I be myself, that I become the self I already am in his eye because he made me, because he made the world in which he placed me, and because he *is* me. When Eckhart blurted out the simple truth, "My *me* is God" and was posthumously excommunicated for his candor, he forever saved me and everyone else from the charge, at least, of *original* sin in what may appear like blasphemy in this statement. The one inexorable and all-comprehensive demand God makes of us is that we become and remain ourselves. In the Hasidic tale, Zusya's guru served him well and faithfully by reminding him that God does not require that he be Moses. He insisted only, but relent-lessly, on his being Zusya. If I fear, sometimes, that the demand may be more than I can bear, I find it in the end just bearable precisely because I am asked only to be myself, not anyone else who ever was or will be.

One fear is a good fear: the fear of losing my desire to be myself. I need not fear sleep or amnesia or anesthesia or insanity or even death, though all are forms of the fear of losing one's self. I need only fear any final loss of the *desire* to be myself. That alone would be death in any ultimate sense. I can afford to trust him, however, who wants this even more than I do, to keep the chance open for me as long as I myself want it. Therefore, I need only fear the loss of the desire to be and evermore to become myself.

There was a folk song with the title, "I Was Born to Be Me"; and a popular song with the refrain, "I did it my way." The pride and even defiant arrogance in the all-too-human assertion this latter song makes is forgiv-able. Judged in the context of human relationships alone, it could be an individual instance of a wilful and destructive attitude. But in the context of God's love, and given obedience to his will, we should be justified, as his children, in returning to him as to a Father and confessing, in all humility and with singular triumph: "I did it my way." We can do this with impunity and with the solace of profound confirmation only in pro-portion as the deepest desire of our lives is to become ourselves for his sake.

Consulting the Unconscious

In our desire to be ourselves for his sake, we must learn to make inquiry on a still deeper level. As modern men, again, we are not allowed to forget that we are "duplex" rather than merely "simplex." We must consult the unconscious if we are to understand ourselves and in order to become the self we have it in us to be. It is out of the unconscious that successive levels of consciousness have emerged. It is also in the collective unconscious that men are not only related to each other everywhere, but remain related to the common heritage of all living things all the way back to the origin of life. It is also the unconscious that bears, darkly concealed, the promise of future levels of consciousness. Hence it is in the unconscious that the past, the present, and the future meet and are in some sense one.

How do we consult the unconscious? How do we engage in communion with the God who awaits there an opportunity to speak to us? We must first become attentive to our dreams. While they are still reasonably fresh in memory we must record the ones that seem significant as faithfully as we can. Here is a no-man's land, which is also peculiarly *my territory*, peopled with ghosts that gibber and squeak in the night. It is a never-never land, but one which nevertheless has an ever-ever quality that is important from the point of view of my quest for self-knowledge. Where can we find the key to decode the strange language in which our dreams speak to us? Freud and Jung and others can teach us some general principles, but we must disabuse our minds of any preconceived idea that we can come by any dictionary of dream symbols and their rational equivalents which would provide prompt and sure-footed interpretations. If a stream of consciousness is experienced as having very great complexity, many things happening at many levels, how much more the stream of the unconscious! We must assume an open-endedness in the message and that it may take months or even many years to understand a particular dream, as Jung himself testifies in his autobiography.

We can develop proficiency in learning to distinguish between various types of dreams. Some are clearly a re-hash of the day's happenings. If there has been intense concentration on reading or conversation, or some visual or sound experience shortly before going to bed, we may experience in dreaming a garbled rerun or extension in improvised terms. These are perhaps the least important dreams; save that if the concentration has been on some creative, original work, dreams may provide the resolution of some problem the conscious mind had not attained, as has often been attested by mathematicians, scientists, and artists. There are also the dreams in which appear identifiable people, often our parents or brothers or sisters and those with whom at one time or another we have been deeply involved emotionally. Here we may look for indications of unresolved dependencies, repressed hostilities, unrecognized fears and anxieties. It is a rich mine offering ore for refinement, especially in the prayers of confession, intercession, and petition, but not excluding praise and thanksgiving.

This is where the unconscious self makes confession to the conscious self and cries out for absolution; it is also where the conscious self must learn that for which it still awaits absolution. If conscious acceptance and self-forgiveness are not at work here, the poison continues to do its destructive work in the unconscious with unexpected and uncontrolled consequences at the conscious level. Edwin Muir, for example, in his autobiography, shares with us a dream in which the guilt he felt as a child with relation to animals, because of the butchering procedures he had witnessed on the farm, found expiation. Many animals, gathered together, lifted their heads upward as if in prayer while a man with blood on his sleeves received absolution from another figure "wearing a robe, which fell about him in motionless folds, while he stood like a column." [2]

There is another category of dreams in which unrecognized figures are role-playing persons we have known or know now. It may be that some unexpressed aspect of ourselves assumes a character and role-plays its own inner needs and desires. Here we are on ground much more difficult of interpretation. A baby may represent an as yet unborn aspect of our own nature, or one still in its infancy. The *anima* or *animus* may appear in changing guise. Repressed sensual passions, hostilities, and anxieties may wear unfamiliar masks and live out in our dreams the lives that are unlived at the conscious level. Here we may look for the roots of autonomous complexes we may or may not have become aware of on the conscious level. Reflection on these dreams may reveal why the complex is autonomous, what we may learn from it about ourselves, and how we can rework the elements of it into some acceptable, viable harmony with our true and best self, the self which springs from and must be kept in communion with the Self within us. The daimon that would lead us into truth about ourselves must be disentangled from the demons that would work our undoing.

There are also the dreams in which archetypal images emerge, sometimes abstract and apparently nonrepresentational, of the kind that fascinated Jung and were identified by him as arising not merely from the unconscious of the individual but possibly from the collective unconscious of the race, symbols pointing at once to the existence of imbalance in the psyche and the way to achieve balance. These may be the most important dreams of all in terms of the message they would impart. From the point of view of the concern earlier expressed, nations, races, cultures should be attentive to what is distinctive in their collective unconscious. And the whole species man may well remain open to the highest common denominator of the various groupings of the collective unconscious for the Word applicable to the whole of mankind.

There are also ways of quickening forms of waking fantasy or twilight imaging in order to get at significant activity in the unconscious. These are not unlike the process of free association on the psychiatrist's couch, except that they involve a discipline of attaining a greater depth of quiet, a centering down, a stilling of thought processes and conscious emotions to a level somewhere between sleeping and waking. Ira Progoff describes it as a going down into one's own well to see what images he may bring up to the conscious level for examination.[3] The material that is produced is very like the material of dreams and can be worked with in the same way. With a little experience it is also possible in this borderline area to sift the wheat from the chaff because here the conscious will is partly involved and recording can be more accurate; but material thus brought to consideration must be correlated with that of dreams, checked against each other. Progoff commends the practice of keeping an "intensive journal" in which the yields of both are recorded in sequence for later study, reflection, and correlation. Again, it is very important, if possible, to work under the direction of, or at least in consultation with either a trained analyst or a mature, well-integrated confessor with considerable knowledge and experience in the field. It is also of considerable help, by way of mutual stimulation and cross-checking, if one can work for a season with a small group of other persons similarly concerned.

The Role of the Body

This is the proper place, I believe, to interject my own growing conviction that adapted forms of yoga can also be of great assistance in this whole process of individuation and integration which we are insisting may be a form of prayer. We in the West, ever since the Reformation, have become too detached from our bodies, putting the premium on the rational process. There is a dangerous body-mind split in us. And Puritanism has made us, at least unconsciously, ashamed of our bodies. I see the adapted practice of some forms of yoga as a means of reacquainting us with our bodies and working a deep-going reconciliation, a very important part of the integration we seek. Yoga may also be a way of praying *with* one's *body;* as we have long recognized the need to train one's mind and feeling and spirit to pray. In our Judaeo-Christian tradition we got as far as postures of sitting, standing, and kneeling, appropriate for various kinds of prayer. But the East is teaching us much more about how certain postures of the body and ways of breathing can induce the deeper quiet and coordination that can at least bring greater physical health and vigor. There is a given and inescapable unity between mind, spirit, feeling, and body; and hence, anything that serves the body's health must also improve every other aspect of one's total being as a person. Witness the phenomenal response to "transcendental meditation" and some of the impressive testimony of its effectiveness in release from drug addiction and in discovering one's own identity.

We have been taught in the West that the body is the temple of the Holy Spirit, but we have been given very little helpful instruction as to how the temple can daily be kept swept and garnished. From want of initiation and practice I can speak with no authority here. But I am persuaded that we need to distinguish the true yogi from the charlatan and to learn what can be applied in a salutary way to our western forms of prayer. And we should not neglect to inquire also of the Hasidic community and other groups how forms of dance may be means not only of corporate worship, but also of prayer in solitude. Surely, David was not the only one called upon to dance before the Lord in solitary worship!

Petitionary prayer at its best is a holy labor to win, by God's grace, interior wholeness. The body and the mind and the spirit are to be brought together again in harmony. The conscious and the unconscious are to be reconciled that they may together glorify the living God. We are summoned in the prayer of petition to find and to preserve our true identity in God.

11

CULTIVATING THE
ATTITUDE OF ADORATION

WHEN THE LOVE between a man and a woman is deep-going there is not only the desire to become one's best self for the sake of the beloved, but also to become one with her or him. The lover feels that he has been recreated, made over, by the beloved. At least hidden potentials have been brought forth and developed. There is also a longing for a deeper identification with the beloved. There is not only the unspoken aspiration: "I want to be me for you," there is also an unexpressed feeling: "I want to be you for me."

Carried to an extreme, this would be pathological projection. As we have been saying, certainly God does not want anyone to be anyone else, not even husband or wife to become the other. The pillars of the temple of holy matrimony were intended to stand apart. Complementarity rather than identity is the ideal Individuality must be respected, even in marriage. It is always wrong for either partner to dominate, even as it would be a form of sickness for either to want to be absorbed in the other. Once again Kierkegaard asks the relevant question. Pressing the point that we must always be conscious of being an individual, he asks: "Even in that most intimate of all human relationships, marriage, are you aware of that still more intimate relationship in which you stand to yourself as an individual before God?" [1]

On the other hand, the desire to be one with the beloved is the psychological counterpart, on the higher human plane of love, of becoming one flesh in physical intercourse. As the prophecy is fulfilled, ". . . and they twain shall be one flesh," so there is also the longing to be of one mind and one spirit. The acceptable fulfillment of this desire is the creation of a new entity, not to be confused with either person, what Martin Buber would have called an "in-between-ness." The person of both remains intact. Both remain conscious of being an individual. Complementarity is preserved, yet something new is created in the union of the two persons, a subtle and elusive entity of which not only the couple themselves are aware but also all those who know them well.

Turning now to the relationship between a man and his God, we perceive that what is forbidden in human love is commended here. Our analogy properly breaks down at this point. Of course it would be wrong to want to become God; that would be apparent madness. On the other hand, complementarity cannot be the objective. We instinctively and rightly recoil from claims like "God is my co-pilot," or "God and I have a good thing going." This is arrogance, presumption, blasphemy. It is legitimate and appropriate and inevitable in the love relationship between man and God to want to lose one's own will in that of the beloved, to want to become like him for the sake of one's self.

All the great mystics attest that the final desire is to lose themselves in God, even to the point that "the eye of the beholder and the eye of the beheld are one eye." This *one-ing* is the consummation of the mystical experience. Yet, at the same time, the life-affirming mystics, as distinct from the life-negating ones, all assert the paradoxical experience that in the very moment of *one-ing* they have never felt so much themselves, so profoundly conscious of being an individual.

The Prayer of Quiet: The Sigh

The form of prayer which gives scope to this passion to become like one's God, to be obedient to his will and to lose one's self in his service, has been variously called contemplative prayer, the prayer of adoration, the prayer of quiet, affective prayer (the prayer of the affections). Perhaps it has been so variously named, as distinct from the general consensus on the other forms of prayer we have considered, because it is so little practiced, and because its practice by relatively so few men and women is understandably so highly individual in nature. Though so little practiced, it may be the most important form of prayer, both for the individual and for the species, as we shall presently see.

The great masters have distinguished two stages in this form of prayer: in the first the person remains the active agent, and in the second he becomes altogether passive. But we shall not here attempt to enter into these fine distinctions. The important thing is to recognize that contemplation differs from meditation. In the latter the mind of him who prays is engaged actively and in a discursive way, under the prodding of the will, attempting to understand the mind and will of God, to think his thoughts after him, to perceive and to accept the implications of his will. In the prayer of contemplation there is a progressive stilling of both discursive thinking and fluctuations of feeling. This is why it has also been called the prayer of quiet. One simply tries to center down and to become still in the presence of God. The only interior act permissible is an inaudible sigh. One trusts that what is to be contemplated will be provided by God himself, whether this is given by inspiration, as it were, or arises out of the unconscious in the shape of images that would impart the Word if we but patiently try to read them.

It is God who is the speaker now, we the listeners. Our posture in much of the forms of prayer we have dealt with thus far may be expressed in the phrase: "Hear O Lord, for thy servant speaketh." Now it becomes, "Speak, O Lord, for thy servant heareth." Now is the real venture of faith and trust. Here, until reassurance grows, we are disconcertingly aware of the critical alternatives: either God is or he is not. Either the universe is alive with him, or it is dead—without him. I am blessed in my awareness of his presence, or I am self-deceived, and therefore of all men the most miserable.

Assuming a patience that is normally foreign to my nature, I await the emergence of images of matter for my contemplation. This is the opportunity I must not neglect if I am to avoid the unfathomable pathos of Augustine's lament: "O Beauty, so old and so new, too late have I loved thee." What is to be encountered in this vacuum that my solitude and centering-down provide, is an opportunity for the emergence of this beauty on its own terms and in its own shape. I may not contrive or force response. I am to be still and await his coming with such patience and confidence as I can manage. "The Lord himself will provide the sacrifice." Note once again a paradox: while images may emerge to which I respond by beholding the fair beauty of the Lord in whatever form he appears, whatever thoughts his presence stirs, as I enter more deeply into contemplation, ideas slip away and images vanish in his presence who is beyond any "idea" of him and remains forever, finally, imageless.

Only God May Be Adored

Before we enter upon that night which is itself the dawn, that darkness which imparts the purest light, we respond to the beauty we behold, in whatever form it is offered, in the spirit of adoration. The affections are involved; hence the designation, "affective prayer." Here we follow the counsel of the proverb: "Man becomes ever more like that which he adores." Adoration is the contemplation of the beloved. The only adoration which is not at the same time idolatry is adoration of God. That is why, though we commonly use the word to express the feeling of the lover for the beloved on the human plane, we ought not to do so. Adoration is a form of love which can safely be directed only to God. Only here may it escape the bitterness of ultimate disillusionment. Adoration may be addressed only to the "holy"; and only God is holy. If a man is conscious that what he adores in the beloved is the presence of God, he may do so, provided he is clear about the distinction between God in the beloved and the beloved's own person. In Holy Communion it is permissible to adore the Lord, whose image the wafer quickens, but not the wafer.

Misplaced adoration is a sin against the Holy Spirit, who jealously demands all of our capacity to adore. Man was given this unique capacity. Or perhaps we should say it is a capacity that has had its greatest blossoming in man. There is an expression in the eyes of an intelligent animal that seems to suggest the presence of the germ, at least, of adoration. But the potential in evolution had to await the development of mind and sensibility before it could become the extraordinary phenomenon it can be in man. Being so important and distinctive a capacity, it can be expected to require employment, for good or ill, even as the sexual drive. As a psychiatrist finds it necessary, in probing for the source of a neurosis, to inquire into the sexual practices or fantasies of his patient, he might be well-advised to look into what the patient is currently doing with his adoration capacity.

Normal spiritual development follows this sequence: when the half-gods go, God arrives. When individuals insist, however, that God is dead for them, we may anticipate that half-gods, if not false gods, will arrive or return. There is a tendency for the energy of this human proclivity for adoration to require some object to latch on to. Another person is the most convenient object. But, as we have seen, there is mortal danger in this, both for the one who adores and the one who is adored. Accepting the role of God for another is as pathological for the spirit as directing toward another the adoration that belongs only to God.

Men may adore a particular style of life. Whether this involves being one of the flower children or a playboy, neither may be indulged with impunity. A Francis of Assisi may be trusted to adore Lady Poverty, but that is because he never forgets that she is only a symbol for him of the Holy Spirit, as is the wafer in Holy Communion. But an embracement of poverty for its own sake can be as disastrous as the adoration of money or the style of life which money makes possible.

A man may adore power in one of its many forms. He may remain blind to the subtle ways in which he is corrupted by it. But his fellows will be aware of these. Who shall be able to avoid being corrupted absolutely by absolute power? Only God. A man may adore his own reputation. It would be better for him if he were willing to become a man of no repute, despised and rejected of men. Adoration directed anywhere else than to God himself finally betrays a man. "What am I now doing with my adoration-quotient?" may be one of the most important questions a man may ask of himself. Perhaps, also, at no other point may he be so readily self-deceived.

God Adored in One's Own Humanity

Here it might be well if we were to return for a moment to the counsel of William Blake that we have already noted in another context:

> Thou Art a Man, God is no more,
> Thine own Humanity learn to Adore.

At first glance, this would seem to contradict what we have been at pains to point out. To adore one's own humanity, is this not idolatry? But see what he is saying. God is no more for us than what we are able to perceive of him in and through humanity. We wouldn't have a clue as to the nature of God apart from the vision of him that has been imparted to us through other men; in other words, through the agency of our own humanity. Even when we think we see him in some other aspect of his creation, in the beauty of sun or sea or landscape, or in some other living creature whether flower or animal, we do well to remember that what we behold is conditioned both by the organ of the human eye which sees and the human brain which contemplates. When we put ideas together and profess that they constitute a vision of God, it is a vision, as far as we can tell, that only humanity, among the manifold creatures of earth, can behold.

The very conjecture as to the being of God has occurred, so far as we know, only to the mind of man. All the intimations as to the existence of God have been mediated one way or another through and into human consciousness. The best wafer, therefore, for any genuinely *holy* communion, resides not in the tabernacle on some altar made by hands, but in the dark recesses, the inner mystery, of man himself. Out of the depths of our own humanity do we come to know God. Therefore, it is finally only some elusive quality or promise in humanity itself, for which we can and should find no adequate image, that must symbolize for us the presence and the power of God.

"But God is more, infinitely more, than anything in humanity. He cannot be so confined," you say. And you are right, of course. At the same time, this very notion on which you insist comes only, within our experience, from the mind of man. No revelation comes save through and to the mind of man. We tend all too easily to forget this, and to pretend that it is otherwise, that revelation is objective, initiated and executed from on high.

"Therefore, unashamedly, thine own humanity learn to adore," that is to say, the God who has chosen to reveal himself in and through humanity to men. He is, of course, closest to us in our own being. He may be adored through the images of him that the living religions have stored up for us. We may contemplate him in and through and beyond these images. We may contemplate his elusive presence in those we love and in those we admire at a distance. But I believe that William Blake is right in directing us to learn how to adore him in our own humanity, at the mysterious core of our own selfhood.

Alone with the Alone

How does one learn to be alone with the alone? First one must seek solitude and preserve a precinct for it in the daily regimen of his life. He must "study to be alone." Next he must brood upon what others who have taken this inward journey have said about it. I make reference to the authentic mystics, the life-affirming ones, in all the great religions. In other words, he must study the maps, as far as these have been charted. We have all laughed at the advice given in response to the query of a certain traveler: "If I were going to go to that city, I wouldn't start from where you are." Alas, we are all too easily persuaded to abandon the inward trek because we are so confident that we shouldn't be starting from where we are. But as with the unnamed traveler to an earthly destination, so with this spiritual pilgrimage: one *has to* begin where he is. There will be found among the maps available for consultation one on which every man bent on the journey can find the place where he is standing, along with a clear indication of the direction in which he is to move if he is to reach his intended destination. If he persists in looking for it, he will find counsel that patently speaks to his condition.

He has made a start. Because he must start from where he is, and no one else is precisely there with him, the journey is bound to be a lonely one. Fortunately, he will find living companions along the way, as well as those who have left general directions for him in their writings. He may at least call out to these, sometimes seemingly at considerable distance, to check directions, to confirm certain landmarks both have encountered along the way, and to find the courage to persevere. But it remains a lonely journey for which the primary vehicle is solitude.

While he continues to reflect upon the best counsel available and consults other contemporary travelers from time to time, he must take his own faltering steps in the direction he would move. No one can do this for him. He must risk losing his way. He must experience the most intense loneliness and be plagued by a recurring sense of futility. He recalls all the dangers of self-deception and the devious motivations arising from repressions that modern psychiatry has warned him of. There are moments when he will be sorely tempted to return to more secure surroundings, lest he lose his sanity. But if he perseveres, assurances will come that he is on his way, assurances that are inward in nature, but can and should be checked with others.

In the meantime, he can be consoled by the fact that he takes this journey not for himself alone but on behalf of humanity. Other species evolve by means of unconscious and what would appear random adaptation to fortuitous changes in environment. Man alone is required consciously to choose what he would evolve into. And the leverage for man in propelling him forward in the chosen direction may well be primarily prayer, especially the practice of adoration. He will become ever more like that which, with the discipline of faithfulness, he adores. He is to discover inside himself, in his own humanity, what he is justified in adoring. When he finds it, he will recognize it and be content to follow the narrow way into life, into greater, richer, life. Even as the Nazarene, who, for the joy that was set before him, endured the cross! And as with Jesus, God himself will be his teacher and guide.

12

COMING TO
TERMS WITH DEATH

IN THIS LAST chapter I want to speak to those who have passed the meridian of life. It would be impossible to specify any particular age because the meridian is reached at different ages by different people. And for most of us it comes and goes before we are ready, consciously, to accept the fact. Several years after it has passed we may reluctantly realize it. The individual knows he has reached and passed it when he finds that he is having to let go of one vocational dream after another, having to accept the increasing limitations of his waning stamina in all sorts of areas, and that he has begun to be more preoccupied with the thoughts of his approaching death than he would like to be.

Arriving at the Meridian of Life

He has been able until now to repress the thoughts associated with his own death with more or less success. But he is now no longer able to persuade himself that "tomorrow will be time enough to think about that." He is vaguely aware that the angel of death is stalking him by the increasing restrictions his doctor places upon him; by his more frequent encounter with fatigue following concentration of effort, physical or mental; and by an unfamiliar awareness that, if he should be called on to die shortly, he may not do it very well, from want of preparation. At whatever age the meridian is passed in the individual instance, I want to suggest that not long after the age of fifty, one should add to his regular discipline a new form of petitionary prayer—that of coming to terms creatively with his own approaching death. This obviously is difficult and, I believe, can be done best in prayer.

In his book *The Divine Milieu,* Teilhard identifies the nature of the need for such prayer and makes suggestions, direct and indirect, of the patterns the prayer may effectively take. He points out that in the first half of one's life one is concerned with activities. Prayer takes the form, largely, of hallowing these activities. The horizons of life are expanding. One is still learning how to husband one's energies and to apply them ever more effectively to the tasks at hand. It is the time of increasing individuation through practical experimentation or imaginative projection into the various roles one still has a reasonable chance of playing. The quest is for identity, for knowing who one really is in terms of vocation and avocations, commitments on moral issues, loyalties in personal relationships. One is reaching toward the reward of realized identity, which is integrity. All of the various forms of prayer we have described will be permeated by the need to arrive at this integrity. To this end one undertakes to consecrate one's activities.

The waxing and waning of energies and capabilities is a very complex phenomenon in individual lives. Probably the peak of physical stamina is reached and overtaken some time in the twenties. The summit of intellectual powers would seem not to be reached in certain cases until the forties or fifties. Certainly one can still be learning a good deal during those decades, still discovering who one is. And it would be impossible to ascertain when one can expect to attain the apex of one's spiritual capacity. We have already noted and concurred in Kierkegaard's observation that one can continue to develop as a penitent even when one is well advanced in years. And some men serve others as gurus at least well into their seventies and eighties.

The only real limitation here would seem to come when the disintegration of memory and reason has begun to set in. Since the pace of ascendency and decline varies with the physical, mental, and spiritual capacities, not to speak of the emotional, only the individual can know when he is called to undertake in earnest this form of prayer we are concerned with now. It is not a case of changing the whole focus of prayer on a particular day or year. Prayers intent upon winning identity continue long after the prayer confronting death has begun; indeed, they never altogether cease. It is simply a matter of proportion, relevant to need at the time.

As a man moves well into middle age, there does come a time when, if he is honest with himself, he recognizes that a predominant and besetting need—beyond learning not to run away from death by repressing any longer his natural anxieties in relation to it—is to prepare to make something creative and beautiful of his own death. Of many things in life it may be said that they may or may not come to pass. Of one thing we may be certain: death will come to every one of us without exception. None of us knows when the angel will arrive with a summons that cannot be gainsaid. When a man has arrived at middle age, he can begin his practice by learning to die well the little deaths of hopes that can no longer be reasonably deferred, of more frequent bereavement, and of deepening loneliness.

Hallowing the Final Diminishment

He has learned by this time that it is not easy to hallow one's activities. It is even more difficult to hallow one's passivities. Teilhard gives us another word, still more poignant, for the experiences that must be offered in this latter state for God's blessing. He calls them "diminishments." Those of us who are living through the middle period of life know what he means. In the progressive diminishments one inevitably dies many times before one's death. But the diminishments have this virtue: not only can they provide new experiences of God in and of themselves, but they can serve as a school master to prepare us for the greatest and final diminishment, death itself.

In death I shall be reduced to dust again. What has taken cellular form in me, the most complex cellular form of any animal, and what has at the same time a unity so extraordinary as to permit personality through individuation, must now return to the merely molecular state in which it abided before the evolution of life began on this planet. The thing I gave my life to, identity through individuation, would now appear to be dissolved forever, as far as any proof to the contrary is concerned.

It is more than the will to live in me can bear. Fears relating to loss of identity are the most intense fears we can know. The fear of severe physical injury reflects not merely an anxiety about pain but even more about the possible loss of identity. Sleep itself requires for the duration a loss of conscious identity. One of the fears that gives man insomnia is the fear of being held in the grip of the dreams that terrify him and that when he awakens he may no longer be himself. The same kind of anxiety is associated for some of us with anesthesia, amnesia, and insanity. What we fear most about death, I believe, is the possible loss of our own identity forever.

But it is not only that we fear death; we also resent it. The idea of our own death as well as that of some one beloved arouses anger in us. There is that in us that rails against a universe in which this has to happen, and against any God who planned it that way. I don't want to lose forever my chance to be myself. Part of this chance is taken from me in the death of a loved one, a part varying in dimensions according to the degree to which I had invested my life in his. And if death be the end of my existence as an individual—and for all I know it may well be—then death would forever foreclose my chance to be myself. For me as an individual, in the depths of my own being, where I know more than anyone else about my aspirations, my secret sorrows in personal failures, and my longing to live an as yet unlived life, there is infinite pathos in this. I both fear and resent it.

When men believed in heaven and hell as specific places to which their behavior in this life would consign them on death, there was also the fear of the unknown outcome. Being confronted by a cosmic judge who had at his disposal the record of the sins they had themselves forgotten, was not a very pleasant image. Only the most innocent or the most self-righteous could contemplate the scene with equanimity. But, unless I am mistaken, this is not really the problem for us. What we fear and resent is not judgment so much as final extinction. Even our guilt takes the form, not of anticipated shame at what we shall have to confess but of the final loss of the chance to live the life we believed we had it in us to live.

Death for us, I believe, has become a symbol of disintegration, of dissolution of identity, the most precious human value we have. This is why we cannot bear to face up to it. We conspire with one another, or at least accept the conspiracy of others, to conceal the reality of it as much as possible. We encourage or allow funeral directors or morticians to make the corpse look as alive as possible and say inane things to one another about how natural and peaceful the loved one looks in the coffin.

Death is natural, all right, and there is a kind of peace, I suppose, in the cessation of the struggle to live. But that isn't really what we mean when we speak in this way. We are making reference to a quality of life because we are not really ready to release the person to the awful anonymity of death, a state in which even traces of physical individuation will swiftly disappear in total decay. So we put death out of mind as much as we can, our own death especially. But the advancing years do not long permit the luxury of the illusion that death may not come if I can only manage not to think about it.

Relinquishing One's Own Identity

The truth is that the only thing I can do is to culti-vate an attitude toward death that will free my declin-ing years from unnecessary anxiety about it. This will be the work of that form of prayer in solitude that I have called coming to terms with one's own death. The first movement of this prayer is, I think, self-evident. I must let death overtake me, in imagination. Let death do its very worst. Let it take our hard-won identity away from us! What we are attempting to describe here is not easy, but it is essential to this form of prayer. It is a kind of practice of dying in anticipation of the inevitable fact. It is a deliberate letting go of my essential me, a willingness to let my very identity be reabsorbed. Since this is what I have always feared more than anything else in the world, in this form of prayer my purpose is to be confronted by it in meditation and contemplation.

We are told, by some who have managed to practice it, that there is a way of bearing intense physical pain by *becoming* the pain, rather than resisting it. Instead of fighting it, if I can take the pain into the center of my "me," if I can embrace the pain with my very *identity,* I can transcend it. Even the little extent to which I have attempted to follow this counsel under physical provocation convinces me that it is sound. As muscular spasm makes pain even more severe, so there can be a kind of spasm of the emotions and will in the inward posture of conflict with pain which succeeds only in making the adversary more formidable. If I can manage an internal "coincidence of opposites," if I can fuse my identity with that of the adversary, the spasm in the areas of emotion and will, as well as muscle, may be relaxed, and with it the pain itself.

I am suggesting that in this form of prayer we may learn how, in some sense, to *become* death. Here is my greatest adversary. If I can *become* death I shall transcend my fear of death. To become death I must cease to be, in my imagination, at least. Paul Tillich wrote a fine set of homilies bearing the title, *The Courage to Be.* That's a good title for the quest of identity in which I must learn to hallow my activities. The form of prayer we are proposing has to do with another form of courage: the courage *not* to be. It has been said that we do not deserve any gift unless at the same time we could learn to live without it. The greatest gift of life is identity. The proverb still holds. In this prayer we are learning how to surrender life's richest gift to its author.

This is the final and great act of trust. It is the only way I can give myself back to God, and really *mean* it. When my identity is drawn through the needle's eye of death I must be prepared for the possibility that not a single knot of individuality may hold. I must accept inwardly my own unmaking, my own radical undoing, my no longer becoming, even my ultimate nonbeing. Perhaps this is the profound message we can accept from the contemporary writers who would confront us with the spectre of meaninglessness and nothingness. If there is any further shore to be reached it may well be by way of plunging first into the sea of nothingness in a spirit of trust. Our twentieth century condition may require even more trust than was required of Job. His plaintive cry was, "Though he slay me, yet will I trust him." Ours may have to be: "Though in death I forever cease to be, yet will I trust him." The purpose of my life has been to realize identity, even unto the degree of integration we call integrity. That has been the burden of much of my prayer. Now, as a final act of maturity, I must be prepared to surrender my identity and to submit to the disintegration, not only of my body but of my mind and spirit as well, my very *me*.

This is surely one of the forms of the dark night of the soul of which the mystics have told us. In their readiness to enter into the *one-ing* experience they have not balked at entering the void. That, too, is an aspect of the universe, and if ultimately everything is one, then man must embrace the death of his own identity, submitting it in trust to whatever the mythical realms of meaninglessness and nothingness can do to it. They testify that when they do this, the identity is miraculously preserved and restored to them, with a mysterious increment: a new sense of its eternal worth. At the same time, there is the knowledge of the paradoxical truth that their identity is merged in an *undifferentiated* unity with everything that is.

This is, of course, the second movement of our prayer, the sense of mystical union with God, a transcending of death through a readiness to die into it, a transcendence which restores one's sense of identity and one's sense of an indescribable—and therefore indefensible—faith that individuality must survive death. It is a faith that is indefensible only in that reason may not support the intimation with argument.

Realizing Ultimate Identity

If man can enter, in imagination, into the great death and really let go of his strangle hold on his own identity, then it will become easier to die the little deaths required increasingly by the advancing years. He can let go more readily of vocational hopes that can no longer be realized, of ebbing physical energy, and even of waning intellectual powers. He can let go of attachments and dependencies which had seemed until now indispensable to the retention of his identity. He is much more ready to part with the *persona* image which he and his friends unconsciously conspired to build and to keep alive.

What we are proposing can impart a great new gift of inner peace and quiet. In his profoundly moving "Ode on the Intimations of Immortality," Wordsworth first laments the passing of the invigorating experience of childhood and youth when his powers were still waxing and his energies could be devoted to hallowing the activities of life. But the poem goes on to confess that something has been gained whose satisfactions are even more profound. He calls it the philosophic mind. The cultivation of such a mind is the third movement of the prayer we are commending. This is the fruit of mystical identification. We can begin to let go of the strain of grasping and claiming things for our own, of the covetousness which is perhaps the last sin to be overcome.

The philosophic mind delights to contemplate the ways in which apparently disparate things interrelate, to establish connections of which one was unaware before. It rejoices in the wisdom that puts various forms of knowledge together into creative attitudes toward life. It exults in exploring a little the place where words come from. It is persuaded that the ultimate character of the universe is benevolent and that it is revealed in the experience of grace. "All shall be well, and all shall be well, and all manner of things shall be well." [1] One need no longer fight time; there is no need to hurry. One can afford to be patient, because the power for good in the universe has been discovered, through experience, to be trustworthy. The philosophic mind has been

largely purged of fear because it has submitted to encounter with the great fear and has not let that angel
pass until he has rendered his peculiar blessing. The
philosophic mind is the mind that has come to terms
with death, even the possible death of one's own identity.

Therefore, the philosophic mind is able to bestow on
one a new dimension of life, the capacity to enter more
profoundly and imaginatively into the lives of others. It
no longer needs to be competitive in achieving, or defensive about maintaining, its own identity. Its peculiar security lies in its having won the identity that is integrity. Therefore, it can afford to entrust itself to the
unlimited pleasures of vicariousness. It can make its
own the vocational successes of others, the recognition
and acclamation given to them. It is free to relive aspects of its own life in children and grandchildren,
whether real progeny or adopted, without endangering
them by unconscious projection. It makes available to
others the resources of its own reservoir of experience
and reflections, but no longer requires the rewards of
acceptance and admiration. It is *free* because it no
longer requires confirmation of its own identity by
others.

God himself has administered confirmation to the
man who has arrived at the philosophic mind in the
depths of his own being, where he is most solitary.
What need has he of any other? He perceives that for
the evolutionary process, which is the form life has
taken on this planet, death is as essential as birth. Life
would not be possible without death. In order to affirm

life he must also *affirm* death. One of the various degenerative diseases which precede all natural death may already be well-advanced in him. It may be bringing in its wake recurring discomfort and pain in varying degrees of intensity. He may have to behold some of the work he turned his hand to beginning to crumble. He may be experiencing successive bereavement of the relationships that have been most meaningful and comforting to him. He will inevitably be experiencing progressive loneliness. But he has never been a stranger to, nor an enemy of, solitude, and he accepts willingly its expanding and deepening dimensions.

His still growing genius is his ability to release his grip upon his own identity without fear and without resentment. He has learned how to die into death. Now he is learning how to die into God, who is the God of the dead as well as the God of the living. At length he is prepared for the last venture of faith, surrendering his own identity, and entrusting it into the keeping of the One who is himself the final and all-embracing identity.

AUTHOR'S NOTES

Preface

1. Teilhard de Chardin, *The Phenomenon of Man* (New York: Harper & Row, 1961), pp. 217-218.
2. *Ibid.*, p. 218.
3. C. G. Jung, *The Undiscovered Self* (New York: A Mentor Book, The New American Library, Inc., 1959), pp. 95-96.
4. *Ibid.*, p. 98.
5. *Ibid.*, p. 99.
6. *Ibid.*, p. 100.
7. *Ibid.*, p. 101.

CHAPTER 2: *Establishing the Ground for Confidence*

1. T. S. Eliot, *The Waste Land and Other Poems* (New York: Harvest Books, Harcourt, Brace and Company, 1930), p. 43.

2. Emma Herman, *Creative Prayer* (New York: Harper & Brothers, n.d.), pp. 26-27.

3. William Wordsworth, "Tintern Abbey" in *The Poetical Works* (New York: The Oxford University Press, 1958).

4. William Blake, *The Everlasting Gospel* (Baltimore: The Penguin Poets, Penguin Books, 1958).

CHAPTER 3: *Assimilating Prayer in Our World View*

1. Teilhard de Chardin, *The Divine Milieu* (New York: Harper & Row, 1965), p. 46.

2. C. G. Jung, *Memories, Dreams, Reflections* (New York: Vintage Books, Alfred A. Knopf, Inc., and Random House, 1961), p. 20.

3. Loren Eiseley, *The Unexpected Universe* (New York: Harcourt, Brace & World, 1964).

4. Teilhard de Chardin, *The Phenomenon of Man*, pp. 225-226.

5. *Ibid.*, p. 227.

6. *Ibid.*, p. 228.

7. *Ibid.*, p. 228.

8. *Ibid.*, p. 233.

9. Henri de Lubac, *Teilhard de Chardin, The Man and His Meaning* (New York: A Mentor-Omega Book, The New American Library, Inc., 1967), p. 132.

CHAPTER 4: *Expanding the Dimensions of Prayer*

1. Loren Eiseley, *The Unexpected Universe*, p. 186.

CHAPTER 6: *Celebrating the Continuing Creation*

1. William Wordsworth, *The Prelude*, Book XI, in *The Poetical Works* (New York: The Oxford University Press, 1958).

2. William Wordsworth, "Tintern Abbey" in *The Poetical Works*.

CHAPTER 8: *Risking Rejection for Deeper Acceptance*

1. Leon Bloy, *The Woman Who Was Poor* (New York: Sheed & Ward, 1947), p. 356.

CHAPTER 9: *Striving to Be a Man for Others*

1. Charles Williams, *Descent Into Hell* (New York: Pellegrini and Caduhy, 1949).

CHAPTER 10: *Working for Interior Wholeness*

1. P. T. Forsyth, *The Soul of Prayer* (London: Independent Press, Ltd., 1916), p. 24.
2. Edwin Muir, *An Autobiography* (New York: The Seabury Press, 1968).
3. Ira Progoff, *The Symbolic and the Real* (New York: The Julian Press, Inc., 1963), Chapters 4 and 5.

CHAPTER 11: *Cultivating the Attitude of Adoration*

1. Soren Kierkegaard, *Purity of Heart Is to Will One Thing* (New York: Harper Torchbook Edition, 1956), Chapter 13.

CHAPTER 12: *Coming to Terms with Death*

1. Julian of Norwich, *Revelations* (ed. by G. Tyrell, London, 1902).